G R E A T
ADAPTATIONS

New Residential Uses for Older Buildings

by Jill Herbers

Foreword by J. Jackson Walter,
President of The National Trust for Historic Preservation

WHITNEY LIBRARY OF DESIGN
an imprint of Watson-Guptill Publications
New York

A RUNNING HEADS BOOK

Library of Congress Cataloging-in-Publication Data

Herbers, Jill.
    Great adaptations : new residential uses for older buildings / by
Jill Herbers.
      p.   cm.
   ISBN 0-8230-2164-5 :
    1. Dwellings—United States—Themes, motives. 2. Buildings—
United States—Remodeling for other use. I. Title.
NA7205.H46 1990   89-22605
728—dc20   CIP

GREAT ADAPTATIONS was conceived and produced by
Running Heads Incorporated
55 West 21st Street
New York, NY 10010

Editor: Charles de Kay
Managing Editor: Lindsey Crittenden
Production Studio: Yaron Fidler
Production Manager: Linda Winters
Photo Research: Kate Struby

Typeset by David E. Seham
Color Separations by Hong Kong Scanner Craft Company Ltd.
Printed and bound in Singapore by Times Offset Pte Ltd.

First published in 1990 in the United States
by Whitney Library of Design,
an imprint of Watson-Guptill Publications,
a division of BPI Communications, Inc.
1515 Broadway, New York, NY 10036

First printing, 1990
1 2 3 4 5 6 7 8 9 / 95 94 93 92 91 90

In keeping with its spirit, this book is dedicated to those who have helped me change and grow and become.

Acknowledgments

BOOKS, LIKE BUILDINGS, RELY ON THE HANDS, MINDS, and hearts of many to become what they are. I would like to thank the architects and homeowners who generously shared their homes and their stories; their dreams, plans, and architectural realizations continued to inspire and nourish the book. I am grateful to those helpful persons who proved valuable at the beginning—librarians, particularly Sally Simms at the National Trust for Historic Preservation, and for great leads to some great adaptations, Margaret Reeve and Joel Granados. To those who listened, and read, and helped me find my way through this book, I am thankful. Among them, Jim Kemp, as usual, offered sage advice and a lot of kindness; Julius Zomper showed that he cared in a way few people can; Joan Iaconetti helped me at a turning point in the project; and my family read pieces of manuscript during Christmas celebrations. I'd like to thank Cornelia Guest at the Whitney Library of Design for her enthusiasm, insight, and common sense. Finally, there are those at Running Heads who worked to make this project a reality: Marta Hallett, who helped me keep my balance throughout; Ellen Milionis, who makes it possible for ideas to become beautifully produced books; Sarah Kirshner, who recommended me for this project; and Charlie de Kay, who gracefully saw it through the final stages. And I would like to thank Leslie Garisto, whose nurturing spirit and editorial instinct helped me and this book considerably.

Foreword *by J. Jackson Walter, President, The National Trust for Historic Preservation* . . . 9

Introduction . . . 11

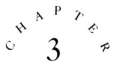

Foreword

ABOUT THIRTY YEARS AGO, THE AMERICAN POET ROBERT Frost penned a couple of whimsical lines that capture the essence of this book. "It takes all sorts of in and outdoor schooling," Frost wrote, "to get adapted to my kind of fooling."

The owners of the remarkable residences in *Great Adaptations* have not only found imaginative ways to live in old buildings of almost every imaginable stripe; they have done so with great style and humor. They have, in short, proven beyond any doubt that historic preservation, often associated with citizen activists in pitched battles with bulldozers, is fun as well.

The adaptive uses in this book are not restorations, although restoration certainly plays a role. They are rehabilitations, which simply means making a building useful or habitable again. The work carried out by these owners shows that there are many different ways to rehabilitate. None of these ways is inherently good or bad. What is important is not so much what is done to an old building, but how well it is done.

The character and charm of all old buildings depends on their details. The owners of these buildings clearly have gone to great lengths to preserve and draw attention to unique features constructed by long-ago craftsmen. In this way, they have become stewards of a small part of American and European heritage.

Robert Frost would have understood the impulse that makes otherwise sane people spend years and dollars making a home from a barn or a city flat from a firehouse. He created quirky and highly individual images through the building blocks of words.

The homeowners of *Great Adaptations* have built unique expressions of personality and style as well. All homes have idiosyncrasies; but these are in a class by itself.

J. Jackson Walter
President
The National Trust for Historic Preservation

Introduction

Architecture is life; or at least it is life itself taking form and therefore it is the truest record of life as it was lived today or ever will be lived.

Frank Lloyd Wright

WHEN FRANK LLOYD WRIGHT MADE THAT STATEMENT, HE may not have had in mind the conversion of nonresidential structures into homes, but the message still applies. Buildings like barns, firehouses, and churches that were never intended to house more than cows, fire trucks, and souls are being made into striking homes for people, and the lives of the buildings are being continued. Many of these structures are architectural treasures; all have stories to tell. As "records of life," whether of agricultural, industrial, or spiritual life, each not only tells something about history, but about the way people lived and worked and interacted.

Beyond their desire to preserve these stone, brick, and wood remembrances of the past, architects and homeowners are turning to them because they fulfill contemporary needs. Some of these needs are purely practical. The rising cost of new housing means that buying and converting an old building is often less expensive than buying or building a new one. Although this is not always true, since renovation and conversion costs can, of course, run quite high, most people have found that the cost per square foot in a large old barn or sprawling warehouse works out to be far smaller than that in a new house.

These old buildings fulfill psychic needs as well. For a generation alienated by the strict and impersonal forms of modernism. After an era in which architects often "started from zero," con-

Coming home to this converted cotton warehouse in Savannah, GA, opposite page, is strikingly different from arriving at most residences. Life inside converted buildings can be quite a departure from standard homes, as well. In a former railroad station in Cornwall Bridge, CT, above, the living room seats are the old wood benches of the waiting area, made comfortable with pillows.

A chapel in Venice, Italy, offered architect Piero Pinto a chance to create a dramatic living space, above and opposite page, with the layering of old and new elements. Stone arches and leaded-glass windows are unique additions to any home, but the contemporary pieces beneath help to produce an unusual effect.

structing visions of the future without reference to the past, more and more people are searching for a sense of history, and are seeking out the graceful detailing, craftsmanship, and care of other eras. Adaptations satisfy this contemporary longing for character and interest in architecture.

The pure originality of these buildings is also psychologically fulfilling in an age when so much is mass-produced, and it exerts a special fascination for those who have grown weary of the familiar forms of urban and suburban housing. Why, after all, settle in a tract house or nondescript high-rise when making a home in a firehouse is far more exciting, or in a tower by the sea more tranquil? Residents of former churches say that no other home could feel so intensely personal. It is perhaps for this sense of intimacy and singularity that these buildings are most appreciated.

Changing demographics are making more of these adaptable buildings available to homeowners. The sweeping societal changes in the latter part of this century have left many schools and churches quiet and empty, and the continued move away from an agrarian economy has driven cows from their barns. It is not uncommon for banks that weathered the Depression to now sit empty on main streets, abandoned for larger, more contemporary quarters. Sometimes, simple shifts in population have caused these once-cherished buildings to be left behind. But adaptive reuse is saving them. After the congregation in a small Virginia town outgrew its hundred-year-old church, the members moved down the street to an old house large enough to meet their needs. A family later bought the church and made it their home, putting life back into the distinguished structure and possibly saving it from demolition. The words of Dale Ahlum, a Pennsylvania contractor who specializes in converting outbuildings, may express the sentiment of the Virginia community: "I don't believe a building should lose its usefulness just because it has lost its original use." A house into a church and a church into a house: These are

valuable lessons of adaptability that show how practical holding on to history can be.

Special Spaces

At first, people may choose to convert an old structure for reasons that seem immediately clear to them: It has architectural interest, or they were looking for something "different" and found it, or they were just drawn to the building the moment they saw it. The charm of these buildings is often instantly apparent. But what unfolds as time is spent converting and living in them is as compelling as what attracted the owners in the first place. Little pieces of the past present themselves in myriad ways, and what becomes evident is a specialness that is uncovered the way stripping away the paint from the staircase of a former carriage house reveals beautiful carved wood below. Often just the physical elements of these structures—how and even *where* they were built—make them worthwhile. Owners may discover after buying a mill house that they can hear the water gently running under what has become their bedroom, or that the fabulous detailing that drew them to a nineteenth-century library is continued in windows that were bricked up and not visible at the time of purchase.

But the deeper satisfaction offered by these buildings derives from the fact that they are already imbued with meaning when the owners come to inhabit them. In a sense, the owners are "borrowing" the spirit of the old buildings for their new homes. And much of that spirit remains. Converted churches are frequently warm and peaceful, and the owners of stables say the buildings have a gentle sense about them because animals lived there. These feelings are partly conveyed by the language of the architecture—the tranquil quality of church windows that carefully let in light, for example. But they often have little to do with the structure itself and more to do with what went on inside it. Even if the pole no longer remains in a converted firehouse, some of the spirit of clanging bells and rushing firemen does, evidenced, perhaps, by boot marks on the floor of the entryway. And the worn spots on the brick walls of stables, where horses rubbed their noses for years, make it hard to forget who used to live there.

These buildings are the ultimate found objects; they take on new meaning as the owners live within their walls and individualize them further. What follows is a look at what the owners discovered—and uncovered—that makes these buildings special and makes them loved.

Living in a converted building often means living with its history. The kitchen of the former railroad station, above, features not only the paneling and wood beams of the original building, but objects and elements from the time of its construction. Likewise, entering the arched doorway behind the wrought-iron gate of the Venice chapel, opposite page, is like stepping into the past.

TIES TO HISTORY   Commenting on the uses of architecture for relaying history, the critic Lewis Mumford wrote: "In a city, time becomes visible." In these buildings, history becomes tangible as well. The years can be felt in an exposed-brick wall or a worn stone floor.

It is these ties to history that inspire a generation with a desire to be reminded of the past. In inhabiting old structures—dwelling underneath hundred-year-old posts and beams and between walls of intricate detailing from the Victorian era—these residents are not just living with history, but living *within* it. There is a pervasive feeling that something has come before.

The designer John Saladino talks about the Roman philosophy of building one element on top of another, creating "layers of history." It is a quite unconscious process in Rome, where several old steps weathered by time may lead to a new building, for example. This preservation of history—not in a museum but in the midst of our daily lives—is the result of converting old buildings, as well. Underneath the veneer of the new is a glimmer of the old, like the icons of angels that are just visible beneath layers of paint on a church ceiling. Every time the owners look upward from their couch, they look at history.

To describe the effect of the old layered with the new, architect Susana Torre uses the word *palimpsest*, an ancient term for parchment that was used and erased when the original text was unwanted, then reused. Intriguing traces of the old text were always still visible—and often legible—under the new. Being able to "read" parts of old structures underneath the new architectural "text"—seeing a smooth plaster wall reach up to meet rough-hewn beams—relates past and present in a visceral way.

Respecting the history in these buildings is the key to a successful conversion, and when the conversion works—when a balance is struck between saving the character of the old and adding the practicality of the new—the result can be far more exciting than anything newly built.

A SENSE OF COMMUNITY   Whether they intend to or not, those who turn old buildings into new homes are not just preserving history, they are also furthering the local community. The most immediate result of these adaptations is that, given new uses, the buildings are not torn down, since they are often the kinds of

Architect Gilles Bouchez converted this forge, opposite page and below, near Fontainebleau, France, into a home for a journalist. The building is so large that the year-round home was constructed within it, leaving the outer part to be used only in warm weather. The glass wall and door create only the slightest separation between the living area and the outer forge. They divide the two spaces physically but allow them to remain visually connected.

structures that would otherwise be slated for demolition. More than that, their very restoration boosts the area and encourages other improvements in what are often interesting, and sometimes classic, neighborhoods. One church in Cambridge, Massachusetts, for example, was converted as part of a rejuvenation of the failing waterfront district; today, old buildings and new sit side by side in the now-thriving historical area.

But most of all, saving and then upgrading old buildings helps keep the community intact on a symbolic level. The barn on the edge of a landscape that lends contour and presence to the horizon continues to do so, only with a renewed sense of life. A firehouse on the corner of a city block can keep giving it interest and a place in history, only now without graffiti and broken windows.

The owners are also creating a community for themselves, something increasingly craved at a time when rushes of technology and shifts in lifestyle have resulted in a sense of disconnection. People are looking longingly back to a time when buildings were part of a neighborhood, not just a row of structures—a time when the symbolic importance of a building like the village church was enormous, and the meeting house on the main street was central to the town's identity. Living in one of these buildings, and making it live again, ties the owners to the neighborhood because they are giving the building back to it.

Because a converted building is a shared building, a more intimate sense of community exists on the inside, where evidence of past lives is found. There is a certain presence felt from the carved initials of children on the wainscoting of an 1865 schoolhouse, the tobacco stains from the smokes of workers in a mill house, or the spots on church floors rubbed smooth from people kneeling to pray. These echoes remind owners they are the second dwellers of a building that once had a place in the lives of others, as well.

AN ARCHITECTURE APART   Beyond the historic importance of converting old buildings and past the sense of community they can offer is an aspect of the process that is of pure architectural interest. Of course, the buildings are chosen—and loved—for their special architecture, but the implications of *living* in them are what prove philosophically interesting. Architecturally, it is nothing less than a radical idea to inhabit buildings that were created for another purpose entirely. It is the farthest thing from the original intention of the builders—or of the building. Public structures such as churches and meeting halls are imbued with architectural symbolism; the vaulted ceilings of churches are intended to lift the spirit skyward, and the massive columns emphasize stability. To live in these buildings is to play with the symbolism and create a twist on their architectural meaning.

The weathered wood floors, beams, and workings of a converted cotton warehouse in Georgia create a surprisingly warm setting for its living area, left. A balcony overlooks the expanse of space that once held thousands of bales of cotton.

The entire idea is pleasantly disconcerting and the result is a quirky charm. Living in a place as reverent as a church, as playful as a schoolhouse, or as utilitarian as a barn produces an effect that no architect or designer could newly create.

Great Adaptations

Part of the excitement of the recent tendency toward conversion derives from the extraordinary range of adapted structures. Not only architects and builders, but individual homeowners as well are transforming structures in the middle of cities, in corners of the country, along coasts and rivers, in backwoods. Out of the thousands of fine examples that exist throughout the United States, England, and other countries, this book can offer only a representative sampling. It stops first to consider what makes these homes special and what they can mean to an owner and a community. The book also offers an examination of the conver-

sion process: finding, deciding on, and buying a building; uncovering its history; and converting it to a place that will be comfortable and aesthetically appealing while retaining the original spirit of the structure.

Rather than giving instruction, this book shows by example what has worked in a number of vastly different and intriguing cases, pointing out elements that unify all conversions, and highlighting the most important, challenging, and fascinating aspects of great adaptations.

The last half of the book is a portfolio of case studies that explores in detail an astonishing array of buildings—from power stations to ballrooms to pigsties. These adaptations are as individual as their former uses suggest, and they illustrate both the practicality and pure joy of making a carriage house, a firehouse, or a schoolhouse into a home.

CHAPTER

1

Researching the Building

THE BUILDINGS THAT ARE CONVERTED INTO HOMES ARE as diverse as the people who eventually inhabit them. The entire process of obtaining and converting these structures is very personal, which is, of course, one of its attractions. Another is that finding and researching a building can be an adventure, and often a lesson in history. Knowing as much as possible going in is not only the best practical approach, it enriches the entire experience.

The Search

Although a few people start out knowing just what kind of building they want, most meetings between buildings and owners are serendipitous. Often, people happen upon a certain structure—a bank, a barn, a seaside tower—and simply fall in love with

it, or with its potential. An architect in Chicago found his church while taking a shortcut home; a couple from Brooklyn happened upon an abandoned firehouse in a quiet cul-de-sac and took the initiative to find out about it. Whatever eventually brought these and other owners to their buildings, it was keeping their eyes open that enabled them to find the structures in the first place.

It makes sense, of course, to look for these special buildings where they are most likely to be situated; in cities, for instance, stables tend to be tucked away in small alleys lined with other old buildings. But just as often, it is a casual Sunday drive in the country that leads to the discovery of a captivating barn behind some hills, or an after-dinner walk in an undiscovered part of the city

that turns up some fascinating historic structure.

These spaces are usually either too special on the one hand or too dilapidated on the other to show up in the real estate pages, although agents sometimes know of their existence. But outbuildings of large estates, such as carriage houses and chauffeurs' cottages, will often be advertised when the estate has gone up for sale. And an old city-owned building, such as the nineteenth-century library that one architect made his home, will sometimes appear in the paper with an RFP (request for proposal) asking for plans for the building's use and a bid. There are public auctions of buildings, too, which are usually advertised in local papers.

In a small town, asking residents about adaptable buildings can unearth them. Small-town gossip being what it is, this may be the surest way to find out everything else about the building as well. Those who do ask may be told, as one architect was, that the church on the hill had closed its doors after a Christmas Eve service years ago and had been empty, except for vandals, ever since. Or, like one family, they may be led to a friendly landmark such as the old dairy barn in Utah that was abandoned despite the town's fondness for it.

Living in a converted building often means being a pioneer: City buildings tend to be found in "undiscovered" towns or neighborhoods, and barns or mills may be left standing in fairly isolated swaths of country after prosperity and the population have moved on. But there are converted buildings throughout Boston, Chicago, New York, and London, as well as many scattered about in thousands of smaller but still-thriving places.

Finding Out About It

The history of a building typically unfolds over time. Its secrets may be slowly uncovered only after someone inhabits it—details may relay pieces of its story, or facts and fables about it may come to light long after it has been made into a home. As architect Carlos Brillembourg says, "It's archeology." It wasn't until the floors were being restored in an old Massachusetts carriage house and newspapers from the 1880s were found underneath them, for example, that the structure could be dated. This kind of unexpected discovery is typical of the often surprising nature of adaptations.

It is wise, however, to find out as much as possible about a building before entering into the intimate relationship with it that conversion usually requires. Knowing about the building's history, site, and soundness—which can mean everything from checking

A converted sawmill in Connecticut, opposite page, is full of new elements that refer to its original use. The shingle siding of the building was stained the traditional brown color of mills, and the small, evenly-paced windows recall factory-like mill windows.

Glass is one of the glories of this orangerie in Stevenstone, England, above. The glass walls and ceilings immediately set this building apart from conventional structures. Built in 1709, it is shown here during conversion—a time when one may have to keep in mind the rewards that make all the work worthwhile.

Architect Grattan Gill converted this Cape Cod carriage house, right, into his family home. Starting with a parking area for carriages that also included horse stalls, a tack closet, and a hayloft, he made a light and spacious three-bedroom space by opening up the center to a three-story atrium and replacing the heavy doors with glass.

The Old Hall in Croscombe, England, opposite page, is as fascinating for its history as for its marvelous materials and detailing. It was built in 1420 as the great hall of a manor house, and was then used as a Baptist chapel for two hundred and fifty years.

its beams to asking the neighbors about it—will better a negotiating position, and make surprises fewer and decisions easier.

Start with the site. Often, one of the attractions of these buildings is their location, such as the old Boston ballroom that sits in the center of the city but is tucked away in a back alley, or the barn situated among rolling hills that reminds its owner of an Andrew Wyeth painting. Because they are not subject to the zoning codes of residential areas, farm buildings and other rural structures are often in places with extraordinary views that are quite a departure from the vistas of suburbia. But because they are, in many ways, odd buildings, they are sometimes in odd places—mills, for example, were purposely isolated, and churches were deliberately set in the center of everything.

If the site is inappropriate, as a last resort many buildings can be moved. But moving historic city buildings may be a violation—

if not of actual regulations, then of a building's place in history and on a certain block. Concerned residents have been known to lodge official objections—and have sometimes successfully blocked an owner's moving plans by court order. This can be avoided by obtaining a valid building permit from local authorities and by determining beforehand that local regulations don't require municipal approval to dismantle or remodel a historic structure.

Barns, on the other hand, are frequently transported to sites that are less isolated than their original settings, and they are relatively easy to break down and move. Indeed, architects have found that the original beams of many older barns are marked with Roman numerals designating their appropriate placement.

Buildings can be moved intact, too, and companies that specialize in this kind of work are easy to find in any part of the country through the yellow pages in the phone book.

The smooth, contemporary look of this kitchen in a converted church in Cambridge, MA, above, is offset by the rustic original fireplace. The simple colors and design allow original elements—such as the delightful cross-beams—to be seen.

This dining room in Dallas, opposite page, contains almost all the wood to be found in this home. A former power station, it is composed of glass, steel, limestone, and concrete. Visible through the glass back door is a vintage neon sculpture that once advertised the wonder of electricity.

When thinking about moving a building to another location, though, it should be remembered that the site is often part of the building's character: A historic graveyard may lie behind a church; outbuildings that illuminate the workings of nineteenth-century farm systems may sit just beyond a barn. So aside from affecting the livability of the building, the site is important because it is often part of a whole.

The next step is to find out about the past life of the building. Some methods to determine the structure's age—examining the nails used in construction, for example—require a professional. Local historical societies, libraries, and state historic preservation offices may have documents, such as old photographs, drawings, and records of the building, that can be both helpful and fascinating. And again, asking local residents almost always turns up something interesting, if only an anecdote about past occupants or rumors of the building's being haunted.

The building's environs are often the best source of dating information. If surrounding structures are similar in style, they can yield clues not just about a building's age but about its construction too. In rural settings, fences, stone walls, and wells can serve as historical markers. Stone foundations generally indicate buildings constructed before the twentieth century; only after 1900 was concrete used extensively as a foundation material.

The most important practical consideration is the state of the structure. Some buildings are remarkably sound, like the mill house in Woodbury, Connecticut, that was about as strong when its current residents found it as when the town's citizens gathered to celebrate its raising in 1707. Others may have their roofs caving in and their doors missing, with only the four walls apparently salvageable. But the structural soundness of a building cannot necessarily be judged by sight. Sometimes there are strong skeletons in a building whose exterior is failing, and sometimes a relatively new paint job or siding material hides serious problems underneath. Barns tend to weather the elements more successfully than other rural structures: Because of their importance to farmers, they were often better constructed than the farmhouses.

It is wise to get expert advice about how much work a building will require just for comfortable living. An architect or engineer can address considerations of loading capacity, plumbing, heating, and electricity. (A list of important questions to consider before buying a building for conversion can be found in Appendix 1.)

It takes vision to recognize what could be a home underneath a falling roof or behind a crumbling façade. But loving the structure goes a long way toward converting it. Good natural light and ventilation are good starts, and any building with adequate space and a comfortable layout for living contains important elements for a residence that may offset minor structural problems.

Considering It

After getting an idea of what the building is all about it is time to weigh its advantages and limitations. First, it is important to determine whether the building can realistically meet the buyer's needs. Those who abandon their search for a carriage house when they fall in love with a barn may have more space than they know what to do with. A family captivated by a church may be wise to ask themselves if the choir loft will provide adequate sleeping space for the children.

The financial considerations are a little more complicated, and depend largely on the individual building. Sometimes the cost of buying and converting an old building is less than that of building or buying a new house. Even when the cost of conversion is higher, the low cost per square foot of larger structures like barns and municipal buildings can make adaptation an appealing alternative. Add to this the possibility of tax breaks, and the advantages are clear. (For information on tax incentives, see Appendix 1.)

The financial disadvantages usually involve maintenance more than actual conversion costs. Old buildings almost always require extra care throughout their lives, even after an initial fix-up, and the costs can add up over the years. Another financial problem

The original floors of a hundred-and-fifty-year-old church in Cambridge, MA, opposite page, lead right up to where the altar was, and where the dining room is now.

The purposely isolated sites of some of these buildings often mean that there is a lot of room left around them. In the case of a garage in Nashville, TN, above, a garden could be planted just outside in a sprawling space that would never be found on a typical suburban lot.

Rough, honest textures—common in conversions—are the main attraction of this coach house in Nashville, TN, opposite page, and the kitchen of a barn in Durham Township, PA, right, that dates to 1850. Builder Dale Ahlum retained the rustic feel in the wood kitchen by using chestnut for new elements like the cabinets to blend with the original oak beams above.

is the high cost of heating oversized spaces. Although additional insulation and the creation of smaller rooms within the structure can help offset these costs, the barn-dweller, for example, can still expect higher fuel bills—or colder winters. It should be noted, however, that most people feel that the aesthetic advantages outweigh the sacrifices.

The physical layout is also important. The fact that these buildings were not made to be lived in is a source of enormous charm. It is also a frequent source of headaches. Some buildings are more difficult than others to convert; barns, for example, do not bend easily to transformation. They often do not come with plumbing, wells, heating, or insulation; they have few windows but far too much ventilation; their walls are not plumb and their floors are

not level. But seeing the charm behind the problems helps. In a stable, for instance, a horse stall may stand in the most logical site for a kitchen, but it is a quaint inconvenience.

A major consideration is the amount of work involved. The truth is that most conversions involve plain hard labor: in a barn, moving a tractor out of what will be the living room; cleaning out the droppings that the average chicken coop collects from 2,000 birds; encouraging wild dogs to leave what has become their home; even handling the clearing of a graveyard from the back of an old church, as is sometimes necessary in England. The buildings are often abandoned and gutted—rotted by time, termites, and neglect if they are in the country, and marked by graffiti and other forms of vandalism if they are in the city.

There are legal considerations as well. Zoning variances may need to be granted to convert the structure for residential use. And buildings of historic interest, particularly those in historic districts, may have a commission watching over them that can restrict changes to their exteriors. The mayor's office can determine whether the building is subject to such ordinances. Though often strict, the commissions will usually work with the owners to devise solutions that fit both their requirements and the owners' needs.

Time is the final factor. Although every building is different, the average time for a conversion is about two years. Some people start to feel that they will end up spending more time away from the building than in it—which may explain why once in their converted homes, people never seem to want to leave them.

Buying It

Buying a building, like everything else concerning the process of adaptation, is an experience unique to the structure. The purchase price may be quite low; the cost of buying a building is almost always less than that of converting it. A particular structure may go very cheaply, for example, if the town or neighborhood cares about it and wants to see it saved and sensitively revived, and this is something to remember in negotiations. Many of these buildings have been sitting derelict for years, and their owners may be happy to have them off their hands. The marks of vandalism are unsightly enough on many of the buildings to keep the price down, but often they do not represent any real damage. Again, it is the structure that matters most, and some sound structures have been known to sell very inexpensively. In the country, unusual deals can be struck that might not occur to someone used to dealing with the formal rules of city real estate: Sometimes the land itself is purchased, for example, and the barn on that land comes for free.

In addressing these considerations, it should be noted that not one person interviewed for this book said that he or she regretted going ahead with the conversion, even with the problems it caused. The process started to become as interesting as the building itself; in a sense, the buildings *became* the process—the product of the hard work and dreams that went into them. And with a few inevitable compromises, the dreams were realized.

Architect Carlos Brillembourg joined two native barns, opposite page, to make one charming home by the sea in Sagaponack, Long Island. All the new parts of the building are painted white to emphasize the differences between the old and new, while enhancing both.

The slanted ceiling of a carriage house, also on Long Island, above, creates a protective nook for sleeping.

White is frequently used in converted buildings to open up the space while creating a light, cleanly designed look. It also often introduces the contemporary. In the kitchen of a former industrial building in Los Angeles, below, architect Frederick Fisher integrated smooth white elements with exposed brick, while in a 1920s dairy barn in Park City, UT, opposite page, converted by architect William Selvage, white is the new outline for the room and wood appears everywhere else within it.

CHAPTER 2
Transforming the Building

AFTER THE EXCITEMENT OF FINDING AND BUYING THE building is over, one is left, often stunned, with the building itself and the job of transforming it. After a woman in Massachusetts bought a Quaker meeting house, for example, she found herself the owner of a big empty room containing three pews—and a lot of potential. This can be enthralling, particularly to architects and designers who see the buildings as oversized blank canvases on which to work. But it can be daunting as well: There is a lot of room in a barn, for instance, to realize dreams. But making a home for cows comfortable for people takes a lot of sensitive planning.

Conversions present two basic challenges: making livable a space *not* designed for living, and retaining the spirit of the original structure while introducing the contemporary elements necessary for comfortable living. These design questions can inspire some wonderfully creative answers.

Whether those answers come from an architect, designer, builder, or the owners themselves is a decision that rests with the individual owner. At the very least, professionals will probably be necessary to provide general architectural guidelines and advice about structural matters. A straightforward conversion—in which old elements are saved and restored, but few major changes are made—can be successfully carried out by the owners, particularly if the structure is fairly sound. But a real transformation, in which

The expansiveness of this former church was retained beautifully, right. The double-height living area is accentuated by the huge original window, which extends to the second-floor balcony. The balcony, which runs all the way around the room, leads to the more private rooms of the house.

the building is brought into a more contemporary realm, is complicated in terms of themes and ideas and will probably be enhanced by an architect. In either case, certain basic problems inevitably present themselves.

Space

There may be too much or too little of it, it may be in the wrong places or laid out in inconvenient ways—space is a unifying problem in conversions. In structures such as carriage houses, schoolhouses, and stables, space may be tight, while in buildings like barns, mills, and granaries, it can be overwhelming.

The challenge is to keep some of the feeling of the original space while making it comfortable and usable. This means maintaining the monumentality and sense of freedom that the soaring ceilings and open volume of barns and churches convey, while bringing proportions into human scale; or retaining the charm and intimacy of a carriage house without its feeling crowded or claustrophobic. It is always better to work with the building rather than against it, to let the structure lead the way when possible. There is plenty of volume in a firehouse, for example; but it is more vertical than horizontal. In such cases, lofts and balconies can make excellent use of the available interior space.

CLOSING OFF   The wide-open space offered by some of these buildings, although attractive, is not very livable in its raw form. To be comfortable, the space must be broken up, physically and visually, while the functions of living—cooking, dining, sleeping, bathing—require privacy and the creation of areas of "separateness." And all of this needs to be done without losing the feeling of openness or, in a barn, for instance, the memory of haylofts.

Architects often approach these spaces as they would a loft, or, when the building is very large, several separate lofts, with the idea, above all, of keeping the space open. Another common approach is to build a structure within the structure, a solution that brings space down to a manageable level and cuts down heating costs. Many architects have mixed old and new this way. A sleek modern box was installed within the frame of a nineteenth-century barn, for example, with large, open spaces in it for views of the original beams and dimpled glass. A more abstract version of the interior box was used in a former ballroom: Latticed walls and partitions were installed to create a "house within a house" for a more intimate atmosphere in the the home's main area.

The interior of the Old Hall in Croscombe, England, above, formerly the great hall of a manor house and then a Baptist chapel, has had minimal redecoration and retained its monastery-like spirit. Each element is displayed without distraction—the log ceiling, stone arches, and intricately detailed windows.

An interesting solution is to move some of the space outside. One builder did this in a barn by carving an outdoor deck out of a large portion of the second floor. It worked for the home in several ways: The interior gained visual interest from the new lines and angles created by the deck. Energy costs were lowered both because there was less space to heat and because the large window opening out to the deck let in an abundance of solar heat. And the owners were left with a huge deck with a marvelous view of the surrounding hills.

The addition of a second floor is another solution, as long as the floor is hanging or suspended but not complete. The idea is to create a separate space without blocking off the whole interior view of the building. Lofts accomplish this particularly well, especially in churches and barns, where they recall choir lofts or haylofts. One converted barn features a whole progression of lofts that descend toward the wide-open living space at the bottom. The higher the loft, the more private its use, so the bedrooms are near the top of the barn, and kitchen and dining areas are closer to the bottom. These "levels of living" are not only practical, they provide the reassuring division of space and the feeling of privacy that most people look for in a home.

OPENING UP   Opening up the space in stables that have beams low enough to hit one's head on, or in stone outbuildings with entrances so small one has to duck to get inside, can be a real challenge. The most common and successful means of making these small buildings work is to use an open plan, which not only enlarges the space visually but actually allows it to function more efficiently. Installing lofts in the corners and on the sides of the interior conserves space and gives the main living area an expansive and luxurious feeling.

Many ingenious design solutions for buildings like firehouses and stables turn this idea upside down: The smaller, more private rooms are placed on the first floors, while stairways dramatically open up to soaring vertical living and dining spaces on top. These upside-down plans take advantage of views and light that are not available on darker, lower floors.

Windows always add a sense of expansiveness, not only letting in light but also by creating views, which bring the outside in. In a New York City carriage house a window wall was installed on

Red neon was daringly placed next to the worn stone of a converted forge near Fontainebleau, France, opposite page.

A new glass top on this barn converted by Carlos Brillembourg in Sagaponack, Long Island, left, lets in light on the patterned space below. The new trellis design echoes the order and pacing of the original wood ceiling beams, and retains something of the outdoors feeling of a barn.

the second floor, opening the space up to a canopy of trees just outside the glass.

Some plans capitalize on the intimate nature of a building to make the small space one of its charms. A kind of "tree house" effect may be the result, with the secluded lofts and alcoves resembling the nooks and secret rooms of childhood playhouses.

ADDING ON   Adding on to the original structure is another way to increase space, of course, but it also allows one to maintain the integrity of the original structure by leaving it virtually untouched. Putting a separate structure next to the original one is always preferable to tampering with the building by adding rooms directly on top or to the side of it. And a second structure can be connected to the first so that the original building still seems to stand alone. When the owners of a former squash court found they did not have enough room, for example, they had a compatible building constructed beside it that is connected by a breezeway. And when the resident of a Quaker meeting house wanted to keep the openness of the space, she had another structure built beside it for living and kept the original to work in; the two are connected by a foyer.

Although it is important for the new building to be sympathetic to the old, an attempt to create a copy of the original structure severely diminishes its integrity. Instead, sensitive and successful additions approximate or are compatible with the proportion, materials, color, and texture of the old building, but have their own contemporary character and design. They are comfortable with the old buildings, but do not compete with them. In many cases, the new buildings are kept fairly simple, so as not to distract from the old. But even if they are a little more adventurous, the lines and forms and spirit of the old building should be followed in planning the new. The most important quality in achieving this delicate balance is respect for the old structure.

The entry to a carriage house in New York City converted by Redroof Design, opposite page, and the living room of a former water mill in Arles, France, above, both project drama. The carriage house gains its striking appeal from the new winding stair and windowed doors that are set against the old brick of the original building, and the pitch of the gambrel roof atop the old water mill creates its impressive lines.

Elements of the old buildings can fit nicely into the structure of the new, blending the two harmoniously. So, for instance, the addition to the Quaker meeting house features new front doors and molding to match the old, and although occasional contemporary elements clearly place it in its own time, as one writer put it, "it is hard to believe it was not always there."

Light

Light is, of course, a big factor in livability. Some of these buildings are bought for their light—a church with windows as high as its vaulted ceilings, designed to flood light into every corner; a squash court that features a huge skylight to provide natural light for playing. And some of the light sources, if not generous, are too interesting to ignore: windows in libraries placed high to protect the stacks of books from direct sunlight; the slats in old Eastern stone barns made for Civil War soldiers to poke their guns through; the wonderful zigzag patterns of windows indigenous to shingled barns.

More often than not, though, light—or the lack of it—is a problem in these old buildings because many were not built with light in mind. Barns can be dark and gloomy; carriage houses are often closed and shadowy.

To find a solution, owners look everywhere for opportunities to bring in natural light. The most obvious answer is the addition of windows—lots of windows, if possible, and large ones, like the big arched window that became the dominant contemporary element in a nineteenth-century carriage house. As all new openings in conversions should, this window continues the play of old and new. Although it is unmistakably contemporary, its simple style does not conflict with the small stable windows on one side of the structure or the big carriage doors on the other. In fact, it successfully relates past and present. In a barn in New York, the original windows—placed near the ceiling so that animals and grain would stay dry—are juxtaposed with big sliding glass doors below that make most of the east wall a contemporary window. It works because the original lines and forms were respected, and because the new windows are basic and do not distract from the old.

Windows don't always have to be created; sometimes they can be "found" in the old structure. Original windows may be hidden,

The French forge is shown here during conversion, opposite page. The rough wood doors were retained along with the spirit of the building.

The lift shown here in a converted cotton warehouse, left, had previously been used to bring bales of cotton upstairs.

Light was not a major concern during the original construction of this former garage in Nashville, TN, below. To compensate, architect Bryant Glasgow used whole walls of windows and skylights to bring light in from every direction and give the space an airy feeling. The cream-colored design scheme also lightened up the shadows of an inherently dark place.

having been covered up long ago when they proved more problematic than advantageous. The owners of a stable, for example, discovered bricked-up windows that were revealed to be glorious both in their detailing and their admittance of light. Looking for elements that might *become* windows is another solution—a particularly valuable approach in a historic structure, since the basic details of the building can be retained and just filled with glass. The tops of big stable and garage doors are often made into windows, for example, or the whole door can have glass inserted into its frame. The stained-glass windows of churches are sometimes replaced with clear glass for more light, but only as a last resort since the original glass is usually so beautiful it is worth trying to save.

When new windows are installed, it is still possible to follow the historical leads of the building. One architect painstakingly reproduced the period leaded-glass windows of his barn—letting in light and a sense of history at the same time. A nineteenth-century firehouse came with a beautiful skylight, so the owners installed others that almost exactly replicate the original.

Skylights, in fact, are a common way of letting light into conversions. Although there are almost entire ceilings made into skylights, the light that pours in through any size skylight can make an extraordinary difference in the interior space below. In barns and other large structures, the living room is often constructed as an atrium underneath a skylight so that both the wide-open space and the light are emphasized.

Sometimes the public windows of these buildings create problems of privacy and light control. Some possible solutions include sandblasting, translucent paper screens, and simple custom-made ceiling-to-floor blinds that let in light—and the outdoors—only when desired.

Usually, it is a combination of solutions that lights up a building. For one firehouse, which was typically long, narrow, and dark, the architects created a central "light well" by hollowing out the center of the building. Then they created an upside-down plan for the house, placing the more private rooms below and the more public rooms above, to take advantage of the light coming in through a large skylight above. They also punched out new windows and installed artful etched-glass panels in the floors of the upper rooms to let light filter through to the lower floors. In this case, it took all of these efforts together to make the building a light place.

The large original double-hung windows of a Victorian schoolhouse in England bring in much natural light, left, but the home was made even brighter with a coat of white paint and the use of light colors in its design. Dating back to 1889, the schoolhouse is still in possession of the paneled walls and formal stair that make it unique.

Views

Many adaptable buildings come with remarkable views, interior and exterior, that need to be emphasized. Interior vistas should show off the most interesting parts of the structure; views to the outside should take full advantage of the often-spectacular sites. Since so many of these buildings are one with the site—whether a historic city district full of other old buildings or a river by a country mill house—exposing the view is part of bringing out the building's character. The scene from the living area of a converted barn, for example, is central to the feeling that the house is part of the countryside, rather than merely sitting within it.

Catching these views often means lots of windows—in some cases positioned all around the circumference of the structure. Sometimes, it just means sensitive placement of a few windows to frame the best views of the landscape, or of elements such as sun porches, positioned on the west side, for example, to take advantage of sunset scenes.

Within the building, lofts, partial second stories, and second-story corridors that pass through the center of the structure allow views of the interior. Standing on a loft in a converted barn and looking out and down, one can recall the feeling of being a child ready to jump from a hayloft; taking in the expanse of space from the hanging second story of an old ballroom, one can imagine the orchestra and dancers below. In a converted commercial building, the staircase leads to a second-story balcony with openings in it made like windows that invite one to stop and take advantage of the open vista.

Balancing the Old and the New

Perhaps the most important—and possibly the most interesting—part of converting an old building is working with the delicate balance between old and new. Deciding what to keep and what to dispense with, what to leave in and what to leave out, can be confusing. The attempt to create a pristine period piece, to use old elements in a contrived way that does not fit the needs or mood of today, in the end insults the integrity of the original structure. What is important is keeping its *spirit*. A respect for the past is important, but it should be a respect that runs parallel to recognizing that what doesn't really work will need to go. These challenges, when met well, can become small architectural triumphs.

The aim of mixing old and new, as architect Arthur Cotton Moore expressed it, is "a dialogue of opposites." It is important

Looking out from the living room of the English schoolhouse, opposite page, visitors are introduced to a glass room that is filled with plants and light. The living room of a converted industrial building in Los Angeles, above, is also a light place, due to its open space and white architectural elements.

The former uses of buildings determine their design. Twig furniture and quilts fit naturally into a converted one-room schoolhouse in Lake George, NY, right. By contrast, the industrial design of a former power substation in Dallas, TX, opposite page, is evident in the new stair railings, which were constructed of steel pipe, electrical connectors, and sheets of wire-reinforced glass.

to see the two contrasting with as well as complementing one another, for it is the contrast that creates the richness often found in conversions. The sleekness of a new plaster wall can be just as smooth as the original brick wall is rough. And the original beams in a barn that have taken on a honey color because of age and wear, the floors that have a patina and polish gained from the threshing of wheat, and the arrises that have been softened by the rub of hay, straw, and sheaves of wheat can sit beautifully under an unabashedly contemporary skylight.

Deciding what in the old structure is possible and appropriate to keep is the first step. In many conversions, exteriors are restored to their original state, leaving the interiors for more contemporary expression. Elements that lend beauty and significance to a building—poles in firehouses, bells in church belfries that can still be rung, and mill wheels turning along the river below a mill house—are almost always worth saving. Original detailing also contributes greatly to the character of the interior: rough-hewn beams, hardwood floors, large-paned windows, even the pipes in former industrial buildings.

If an important element in the building must be removed, a sensitive architect or homeowner can usually find a way to replace it with something new that at least nods to the past. When a church vestibule obstructed the layout of a home, for example, the architect removed it but used the vestibule's outline as the basis of a new addition.

Old parts of a building can often be salvaged with help from contemporary pieces. The owner of another church wanted to save the heartwood floor that dates back to the nineteenth century, but it had rotted in very visible places, like the entryway. So she scattered contemporary decorative tiles in the damaged spaces. Looking like a free-form contemporary design, they do much to introduce a contemporary sensibility into the old church.

Contemporary elements are often the answer for saving such elements as old entryways that contribute a great deal to the character of the building despite their lack of practicality. Many old sliding barn doors, for instance, are too large for people to enter and leave through on a daily basis. But the building is unimaginable without them, so often a smaller entrance is carved into the large door.

When original details are too impractical to keep but too charming to give up, a common solution is to reuse them in a different way. This idea has special appeal because, on a smaller scale, it echoes what the owners have done in converting the building—recycling the old to make it work in a new way. The owners of an 1890s firehouse, for example, removed the rows of slate shower stalls they found on an upper level and used the material to construct a new, sleek fireplace; the planters on the back terrace were made from the wainscoting that had to be removed from the front of the firehouse. In a former barn, oak, ash, honey locust, and poplar slats from the old corncrib were used to make new balusters for the stairway and balcony, and the flooring was made from the old barn siding.

Often, the appeal of completely new elements is that they are strikingly different from what is already there, but they should still flow naturally from the original architecture. So if the forms are not alike, the materials might be complementary, or if the

An unmistakable former barn outside Washington, D.C., below, houses a large family. New walls were built around the old so that the original framing, siding, and roofing could be seen and celebrated from the interior. The original stone walls and floor date to 1840, but modern innovations such as the rooftop solar collectors bring it up to date.

materials are different, the colors might unify old and new. The interior may be very contemporary with echoes of the past, and old elements may show through the new like ghosts in the house.

In many buildings a single, particularly strong element introduces a contemporary sensibility—a sleek, steel staircase, perhaps, or an exterior piece such as the gridded tower that was added to bring together two old Long Island potato barns.

The fun of living in a building that used to be something else can be expressed in new details that comment on the structure's original function. A converted barn in Massachusetts features a new second-story sun deck built in the shape of a silo, complete with bands of steel. And one architect had small wooden horses' hooves carved on the exposed rafters of an old stable to remind the new residents of the previous ones.

In talking about a barn that his firm transformed into a home, architect Yann Weymoth summed up the exciting interplay of the present and the past: "We've made the contrast between old and new deliberately clear. And I think both benefit from the juxtaposition of soft and hard, warm and cool, textured and smooth, romantic and classical."

Designing the Interior

In many of these buildings, the architecture is so interesting, the detailing so compelling, that the interior designs itself. Indeed, sometimes the architecture *is* the design. The drama of the windows or the presence of an intricately carved oak staircase, ornate patterns on a tile floor or a tin ceiling may strikingly dominate an interior. In this case, simple furnishings are best for allowing the elements that make the building special to show, and additions can be kept to a minimum—plain ceiling fans in a church, for example, or the irony of a fireplace in a firehouse.

But there are more involving ways to handle the details of interiors, too. One is to extend the character of the building to the design, furnishings, and objects within it. Because barns relay a sense of craftsmanship, for example, furniture from the Arts and Crafts and Mission movements is often used in them; the simple, honest lines of these pieces naturally relate to those of barns. In a Nashville coach house, the rusticity of the brick exterior was taken indoors with "rough" elements such as dark paint, exterior shutters for the inside windows, and wrought-iron staircase rails that serve as curtain rods. And in former industrial buildings like the Dallas power station that was converted into a contemporary

The simplicity and formality of the interior of an old church have been elegantly retained with traditional furnishings and objects that reinforce the order and pacing of the original paneled doors, clean lines of the windows, and weathered floors, left. A large plant, however, lends the room a contemporary sensibility and an air of liberation.

home, steel, glass, and other industrial materials may be used to echo the Machine Age background of the building; the color palette, too, may be more industrial than domestic, consisting of grays, blacks, and metallics.

Again, it would be a mistake to try to replicate the past in an old building, because the result would be a period piece that seems contrived. Designer Leslie Claydon-White expressed this sentiment well when he said, "I do not want my home to look like a museum." So although he chose paint, wallpaper, and hardware to correspond to the period of the mill house he converted, the furnishings and objects are an eclectic mix, ranging from antique to contemporary, American to Far Eastern. And it all works.

Completely contemporary approaches can also work; they gain a certain intrigue from existing against the backdrop of a historic building. In an ancient forge in France, for example, bright neon lighting and daring abstract furnishings strikingly emphasize the aged stone walls and measured bricks of the building. There is a pleasant degree of shock at the contrast, then a sense that old and new can live together comfortably in the same building.

These spaces are often filled with found objects because adaptations are, in a sense, just large found objects, old pieces serving new purposes. The chairs in one converted church, for example, were made by cutting down the original pews, and the sign outside the church was taken indoors and mounted on industrial pipes to make a coffee table. In a Long Island barn, table bases are cast-iron flywheels, and a hay trolley is suspended among the rafters for decoration. Ornate windows and marble mantels salvaged from other buildings, a cast-iron winding staircase taken from a bank, the lights from a railroad car that became a chandelier, an iron cooking kettle that now functions as a bathtub, and the donkey saddle serving as a magazine rack in a converted stable—all of these are examples of found objects that can make the rooms of a converted building complete.

Most owners find that their conversions as a whole, and the specific interior elements in particular, are much like cathedrals—ever-changing and never really finished. Much of the design evolves over time, and owners should not panic over it during the first few months of living in the building. For most owners, this evolutionary approach is a joy rather than an inconvenience because the whole experience is a process, an extension of the sense of discovery that first brought them to their great adaptations.

The milking parlor of a Utah barn, opposite page, was made into a living and dining area, which captures the light on this level. The sleek white stair rails are juxtaposed to the original beams, and the small windows, although contemporary, are modeled after the openings in barns that were made big enough to provide ventilation but small enough to keep out rain.

To stay true to its background, the colors used in converting a Dallas power station, above, are more industrial than domestic.

A classic barn with an "English" style framing structure underwent a beautiful transformation. The barn's ceilings are twenty-seven feet high, supported by original gunstock columns still visible inside the home, opposite page. After being turned ninety degrees, the structure, left, was backed with a truck onto a new foundation, which contains a lower level.

CHAPTER 3
Creative Conversions: A Look Inside

Tin Roof Barn, *Vermont*

When architect Peter Woerner came upon a barn in Vermont that he could not turn his back on and decided to make it into a home, his first objective was to show off as much of what was left of the 150-year-old structure as possible. What was left was worth saving—and showing: a frame that went out of style in the 1830s composed of a tin roof, a continuous forty-foot beam that runs the entire length of the barn, hand-hewn wood gunstock columns that stand sixteen feet high and support the frame, and an intricate system of interior beams that cross and join in perfect symmetry.

While the approach of many architects to barn conversions is to build a new frame inside the old structure, Woerner took the opposite tack and brought the outside *in*. He enclosed the old frame and ceiling inside a new "envelope" of exterior walls and a roof

so the entire pristine frame is visible within as a free-standing structure, making it possible to see and live with the original elements inside the barn house. When one looks up, there is the original—and rusted—tin ceiling and the beautiful old columns with intricate detailing, exposed all the way down the structure.

The barn, which stood on land belonging to some friends of the architect, had probably not been used since World War II, judging by the profuse vegetation that had grown up all around it. In fact, it might have rotted completely in another ten years. Like many old barns, it was abandoned after the economy changed in the postwar years. And like many old abandoned barns, it required a good deal of work to make it livable.

When Woerner found the barn, he was growing tired, he said,

of producing slick, perfectionist projects, and "wanted to get his hands dirty." He did. First he had to clear away the dense woods around the barn to be able to work there and get any kind of view. Then he undertook the ordeal of moving the structure—just ninety degrees. There were a number of reasons why moving a thirty-by-forty-foot structure with a delicate frame actually made sense. With barn conversions, it is usually necessary to dig under the barn to create a new foundation, since the original foundations were not constructed with living in mind, and they allow the barn to shake. By moving the barn, Woerner could simply turn it onto a newly laid foundation. And because the land sloped downhill to one side, there was room for Woerner to add another, lower story to the house, in the new foundation. In addition, with the barn facing ninety degrees in the other direction, the view was better, something that was not taken into consideration for the sheep who were living there before Woerner.

To move the barn, Woerner had it set up on steel beams, turned ninety degrees, and driven with a truck onto the new base—which was now the first floor. He made the foundation one foot wider and longer than the frame so that he could wrap walls around it, creating the new envelope. With the newly created lower level, the barn became a traditional "bank barn," where one can enter either on the new lower story or on the original first floor where the bank rises up to meet the original entrance to the barn.

The new lower level holds two bedrooms and the garage, and the main "public" rooms are in the original barn space above. Inside that space is the beautiful original barn structure—exposed beams, ceiling, and rafters. But the frame is not all that Woerner brought inside. He brought in the spirit of the original structure as well. The new elements reflect it—rough plaster walls that maintain a rustic feeling; windows that, even in their contemporary candor and oversized stretch across the structure (necessary in such

New spruce siding, which matches the floors inside, was placed on the barn, and cedar shingles were laid on top of the old rusted tin roof, right. The spacious structure is surprisingly economical to heat because Woerner made sure that it was very well insulated. "Low E" insulated glass was used for the new windows and glass doors.

a large building to keep things in scale), are simple and ordered in a way that honors the architecture of the barn; a stone fireplace that is so much in character it looks like it just formed there.

The interior is as honest as the frame itself, relaxed and unpretentious, but impressive because of its soaring volume. Woerner wanted to retain the feeling of loftiness, so he left the main living area open to the rafters. But lower ceilings installed over the transitional entryway and other areas like the kitchen create warmth and keep the building from overwhelming its inhabitants. In addition, original seven-foot beams run overhead along the length of the barn, so there is space all around but a comforting feeling of enclosure just above. Atop it all hangs a sleeping loft, enclosed by walls and windows that give it the look of a little house and make it popular with children, who love to play there.

Even the furnishings seem to be a natural outgrowth of the barn structure: The coffee table was made from a sled, found nearby, that was used to carry tools and supplies around the farm; a ladder that came with the barn and probably went to a hayloft was left in place and now goes delightfully nowhere; a swing hangs from one of the beams; and paintings, toy trucks, and various curiosities sit on the rafters, completely at home.

In making a ramshackle barn into a real home, much had to be disposed of, but what Woerner held on to was a sense of honesty inherent in barns. The rough textures, the weaving together of simple materials, and the straightforward structure all meet to convey a true spirit of craftsmanship, and a human element made apparent by that sense of craft.

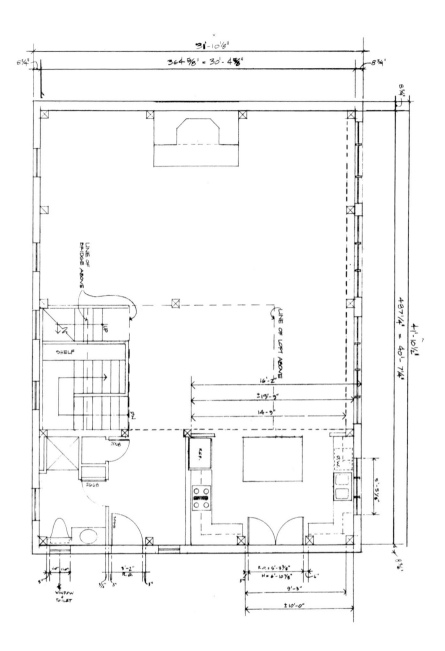

The loft above the main living space is more private than one would imagine, as there is so much room in the structure that the loft is barely noticed, above. The kitchen and bathroom are fit into the corners of the building so that the remaining space could be kept open. French doors open off from the kitchen onto a flat grassy area that provides an outdoor dining area in warm weather.

Firehouse, *Brooklyn, NY*

"We just saw space," is how Janet and Walter Kenul describe their reaction—and attraction—to a firehouse in Brooklyn that stood abandoned and rotting and waiting to be saved. Space was about all there was to see in the hundred-year-old building, with the exception of rotting beams, falling plaster, and broken windows. Even the brass pole was gone, stolen by scavengers. The firehouse had been sitting lonely for ten years, except for visits from vandals, who tore up what little they could find on the interior and covered the exterior with graffiti. The rest of the damage was done by rain that poured in through broken skylights.

Today, the old firehouse is a beautiful, comfortable, contemporary home that still looks to the past in a friendly way. And it is not just the big front doors where the trucks used to rush out that remind the owners of what the building used to be. Longtime residents of the neighborhood who remember the engine company with fondness come by to recall school trips to the fire station, and some of the old firemen themselves drop in from time to time to see what has become of the place.

When the couple set out to find a building to transform, they were looking for room to expand and a special structure that would suit their needs and visions. As artists, they wanted a place to work and show their art, as well as to live. When they found and fell in love with the firehouse, they went to the city registry to get information on the owner, but could not track him down. By coincidence, they later visited a realtor who had been hired by the owner, and who put them in touch with him.

The 1890s firehouse, opposite page, sits on the last block of a main street in Brooklyn. The ironwork in the front was added for security and decoration. The inside, left, is bright and airy. A new steel spiral staircase leads to a small bedroom above the top floor of the home.

Next, they did what is typical—and inevitable—for many who convert buildings: They bought the building only to gut it, because so little of the interior structure was of use. As it turned out, the politics of getting approval for codes, regulations, registrations, and all the other paper work required for altering the building was harder than working with a sledgehammer to knock down walls or carrying the rubble away in a wheelbarrow, which they did for months to hollow out the building.

An architect was called in to tell the Kenuls what they *couldn't* do, but they orchestrated the rest of the conversion. Walter Kenul had a good deal of carpentry experience, and the couple relied on trade-offs with friends and acquaintances—the slick cabinets that help define the kitchen were made by a friend who took their jeep in return, and many of the other new elements are material representations of favors that were owed or exchanged. The whole project took three and a half years; after the first two years the couple moved in and continued the conversion.

The exterior was restored using hydrochloric acid, to clean off the graffiti, and the favors of friends who knew welding to make a gate for the entryway. The large "38" signifying the number of the engine company and the brick "BFD" ("Brooklyn Fire Department") are still charmingly in place.

On the interior, the Kenuls basically followed the building, letting themselves be guided by its lines. The exposed-brick wall on one side of the building and the carved staircase that runs alongside it are the only original pieces that could be left in place. But anything of interest that had to be torn out—original doors, windows, and trim—were used elsewhere throughout the house, creating a sense of continuity with the past.

The first floor, once the home of the horses that pulled the fire carriages in the early days of the firehouse, now holds a large apartment; eventually the Kenuls plan to "live into" the space, using it for a studio, workroom, or gallery. Up the oak staircase, which ascends through the whole building, is the main floor of the home, with an entryway, dining room, and kitchen. Here one begins to see how the owners have created their own architecture with sculptural elements and smooth surfaces. The area is a study in slate, a material that the Kenuls found by the pound in the fireman's shower stalls on the top floor of the building. They tore out the stalls and used the slate to cover much of the surface area in the house—the kitchen counter, the floor of the terrace opening

Slate is a dominant element in the design of the home, covering everything from the kitchen floors to the dining table. The new back terrace opens off from the kitchen on the main floor, opposite page. Also on the main floor is the dining area, above, reflected in the mirror that one of the owners made from found objects such as columns and fence tops. The sculpture visible in the mirror was made from fire-fighting hooks found in the basement. To the left of the mirror are original doors and cabinets fronted with frosted glass that were torn out of places where they could not be used and restored.

A pre-conversion shot of the firehouse, right, shows its dilapidated state—broken windows, falling beams, rotted floors. Everything that could be saved, such as the doors stacked here, was repainted, restored, and used somewhere else. Heating the building can be quite expensive, but in converting it the owners used insulated glass and other forms of insulation to keep as much heat in as possible.

off from the kitchen, even the dining table. Though the slate itself is probably more than a hundred years old, its cool black surface takes on a sleek contemporary look when placed among the other contemporary elements in the house. Other pieces of the old structure, used in new ways, are everywhere in evidence: The new terrace off the kitchen holds planters made from the wainscoting that was torn off the front of the building; original frosted-glass windows and doors were repainted and used for cabinets and doors to other rooms opposite the dining area.

Upstairs, the living room and the loft bedroom are washed by natural light from the close spacing of the original windows and the new skylight above, which approximates the one that was broken. Here, the straightforward lines of the firehouse melt into sculptural space: The new walls curve and undulate, and the loft that holds the bedroom is reached by a rounded stairway (a contribution from an architect who used to work for I. M. Pei). And the

ceiling drops and rises in different places—both to visually separate the living area from the main bedroom and to allow a small bedroom on the third story (reached by a new steel spiral staircase) to have a dropped floor.

The element that best sums up the house sits against one rounded wall—a fireplace made from the abundance of slate and installed in the shaft once used to dry the firehoses. In addition to helping keep the large space warm in the winter, the fireplace adds a nice irony. Building on what Janet Kenul calls "the protective spirit" of the firehouse, the Kenuls have created their own expression of a home. They hold art shows in the space, and the pieces made from found objects—a mirror fashioned from columns and fence tops, a sculpture she made from firefighting hooks discovered in the basement—reflect the spirit of "found art." So does the house itself: "This is just another form of our art," Janet Kenul says. "It's the biggest piece of artwork we've ever done."

The original oak staircase that leads to the top floor of the home, left, was stripped and finished to let the marvelous carving show and to pick up the tones of the wood. The rounded element across the room hides a stairway that leads to the loft bedroom. The space under the bedroom is used for closets and storage. An original skylight is one source of heat; the fireplace made from slate found in the building and installed in the shaft once used to dry firehoses is another.

The interior of the tower is most striking for its arched forms and white-washed brick walls, but new elements add to the intrigue, right. The stair-way, newly constructed from unorthodox materials such as scaffolding poles and yacht rigging, brings the home a contemporary finish, which complements its intrinsic roughness.

Martello Tower, *Suffolk, England*

John and Suzanne Fell-Clark were buying fresh fish on the Suffolk coast in England one day when, as Mrs. Fell-Clark tells it, "John pointed to this huge pile of gray bricks and said that it looked interesting." That was the beginning of an adventure, for the pile of bricks turned out to be a Martello tower, one of 103 built and only forty remaining. When the couple went down the shore to explore it and climbed up to look into a small window, they decided they wanted to make the 750,000 bricks into a home.

The Martello towers (named for Mortella, a cape in Corsica where a similar tower was attacked by the British navy in 1794) were built between 1805 and 1810 to ward off the Napoleonic invasion that never happened. After that, they were used as lookouts against smugglers from Holland and then, during both world wars, attackers. When World War II ended, the towers were sold off. The Fell-Clarks bought theirs from a farmer who owned the surrounding land.

The building *looked* like it had been attacked—on the inside. A leaking roof left pools of water lying everywhere; the water had rotted the main floor, which was falling in, and much of the brickwork. What was left was a very impressive shell—round walls made of layers and layers of brick, some of them nine feet thick.

The first step toward making the tower livable was to dry out and waterproof the inside. Over three months' time, huge dehumidifiers sucked out one thousand gallons of water. Then, to keep it dry, the entire building had to be regrouted. The original design

Martello Towers like the one now inhabited by John and Suzanne Fell-Clark, above, are officially recognized as ancient monuments. In fact, the novel *Ulysses* begins in one. When the Fell-Clarks said that they were "looking for something unusual," they were certainly in earnest. "Here," they say, "we feel invisible to the rest of the world."

helped in this regard; ventilation shafts throughout the building, originally built to keep cartridges and shells dry, help the air to circulate.

John Fell-Clark, a designer, drew up plans for the house—a challenge since the tower has no corners. After an architect translated his plans into a final draft, the conversion began, headed up by a builder who was also the local undertaker. Though the original windows in the building are charming, there are only five of them and none are on the first floor. The sun reflecting off the sea and into the house provides some light, but not enough. Installing new windows in nine feet of stone would have proven enormously difficult—and would certainly have compromised the character of the building. So to lighten the place up, the entire inside was painted white.

The owners wanted to "get the full circular feeling of the tower" and allow the architecture to show, so they kept the interior simple and added on as little as possible. Not that English Heritage, the strict historical commission that oversaw the conversion, would have let them do it any differently; they did not even allow nails to be hammered into the bricks—they had to go in the mortar between them.

Although the ceilings in other parts of the tower reach up to twelve feet, on the first floor they drop down to seven feet in places. Here, two bedrooms have been placed in what were once storage alcoves for powder kegs; they are tucked into the house like ship's cabins, compact and unobtrusive. And the gunpowder room became another kind of powder room—the bathroom for the first story. One of the only separate rooms in the tower, it was made to be closed off to contain possible explosions.

The second story, which originally held the officers' sleeping quarters, was left open, and furniture is tucked away as much as possible so that the building can show without interference. Cabinets and beds that pull out at night are built in along the curving walls. The dining area, kitchen, and main bedroom are up here, among an original stone fireplace, 180-year-old flagstone floors—a material used to contain possible explosions—and the massive central column that reaches up to the vaulted ceiling and supports the entire roof. The new staircase consists of materials, that, like many used in the house, were ingeniously scavenged. The banister and handrail consist of scaffolding poles painted white and framed, then filled in with stainless steel yacht rigging. The joints in the poles make for their own distinctive design. The lamps that illuminate the central column and bring light to the whole floor are also made from scaffolding poles—with a lightbulb at the top. The dining table is a slab of marble placed on top of a drainpipe. Even the outside entry stairs were fashioned from old fire escapes.

The roof is an environment unto itself, more comfortable for living than one would expect at the top of a tower. Along with old cannon barrels sits a glass house that makes it possible to use the space when it is cold. The house was put up with a crane in the face of strong gales and it is amazing that it survived—and remains, even in very high winds. Up there, the owners can see around for miles, and most of what they see is ocean; they have few close neighbors, and the village is down the road.

When the Fell-Clarks enter their home through the original oak door with the huge iron bar across it, they feel as though they have escaped to a safe place. Upstairs, when there is sunlight, ripples reflected from the waves show on the vaulted ceiling. And although the owners can hear and see the North Sea from there, they feel singularly protected from it—and everything else.

The original flagstone floors on the second story, opposite page, were used to contain any explosions that might occur in the tower. The huge column that supports the structure, left, provides a dramatic centerpiece for the main area of the house. Furnishings here are unpretentious—finds from local sales, family heirlooms, antiques.

Because the house is essentially round, interior design was sometimes a challenge. A minimalist approach was taken so that the fine original elements of the tower would be allowed to show, right. Even the heating system is covert so as not to interfere; cables under the floor and a large open fireplace in the living area keep the space warm.

The dining area under the curved stone ceiling makes a cozy setting for entertaining, left. Looking out of windows from the tower, above, is an event since most of them are preceded by several steps. The windows were designed for the use of men keeping watch and their guns rather than as a source of light.

Schoolhouse, *Lake George, NY*

"It was just a vacant rectangle," says Joseph Vallone of the hundred-year-old schoolhouse he converted in the Adirondack mountains of New York. In fact, the building's simplicity—its classic shape and straightforward lines—was what drew the architect to it in the first place. He and his wife, Caryn, have made the rectangle into their home, taking care to retain its structural honesty as they did so.

The one-room schoolhouse, sitting on a knoll overlooking the Hudson River, was built in 1894 with $400 raised by the community—certainly a good deal less than it cost the Vallones to convert it. They bought it, appropriately, from a schoolteacher who lives next door, and they do not have to look far to find connections to it. Their cabinetmaker's mother-in-law used to teach there, and all sorts of people stop in to take a look at what happened to the building they went to school in. Vallone says the community was a little nervous when workers took a chain saw to the severely damaged roof, but they were impressed with the final result.

The building was in singular disrepair after sitting empty for two decades. Little was salvageable but the basic structure—and a bell. Vallone began making it livable by replacing the leaking tin roof, first raising the slope of it two feet to allow room for a loft bedroom inside and increasing the overhang to hold the snow and protect the lower part of the building outside. It was finished with copper panels, which are reminiscent of those on the original roof and are already aging to a fine green patina.

Next, the walls were widened to ten inches to make room for added insulation against the cold Adirondack winters, and the rotten pine clapboards were torn away and replaced with new siding. The final improvement to the exterior was an entrance portico that is an echo of the larger structure—a little gable-roofed square that helps keep out the cold and makes the building more like a home by creating a formal entryway. The classic school bell was removed, sandblasted, polished, and reinstalled in the bell tower. A light in the tower makes it shine at night.

The interior required as much work as the exterior. A kitchen, bathroom, new windows, plumbing, and wiring all had to be added. And the space needed to be divided up to accommodate the different functions of living. Vallone kept to an open plan to retain the one-room spirit of the building, creating separate areas for living, dining, and cooking with the placement of furniture and lighting. The only room that is closed off is the new bedroom in the back of the schoolhouse.

Though the cathedral ceiling was one of the attractions of the schoolhouse, Vallone felt that its height might prove overwhelming. To bring the space into scale and introduce a sense of comfortable enclosure, he ran an oak beam above the door all the way around the walls of the structure. The oak complements the pine of the original wide-plank floors.

To open up the small space—850 square feet in all—Vallone put in sliding-glass doors on one side, which lead out to a new

Joseph Vallone took advantage of the building's cathedral ceilings to add a loft at the back, below. It presented an opportunity to introduce a contemporary sensibility in the turn-of-the-century structure. The loft is fronted with glass for a modern transparency, and the top of the black steel ladder used to reach it is a pool-style design.

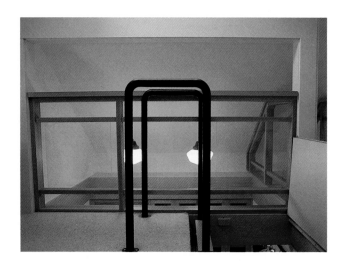

deck. He also used lots of windows, most of them patterned after the sensible-looking schoolhouse originals. But some are contemporary complements—straightforward and classic—most notably the large round window high above the front door. Because of its placement to the south, it lets in light all day long; at certain times of the day the light flows all the way to the back of the house.

The rest of the interior is carefully designed to allow the character of the schoolhouse to shine through. Although the original chimney had to be removed from the back of the building to make room for the bedroom, a new chimney was built on the side, and a wood-burning stove keeps the home warm in the spirit of the nineteenth-century structure. The school's blackboard was saved and now serves as a message board in the kitchen. And new slate was used throughout the home: on the kitchen counter, the floor of the entryway, the hearth of the woodstove, and the sinktops in the bathroom. It is an unexpected material, one that brings to mind blackboards and lessons while looking sleekly contemporary. The same play of old and new can be found throughout the interior: The Vallones were able to retrieve the original school desks and even the large colorful pull-down map from a local antiques dealer, and these and other antiques sit comfortably among the smooth, contemporary lines of the black bar stools in the kitchen, the pool-style ladder going to the loft, and the loft itself, fronted with oak-framed glass and topped with a skylight.

Although a vacant rectangle was all the building seemed to the Vallones when they first saw it, its bookish lines and structure kept asserting themselves during the conversion. And the schoolhouse spirit remains. Because of the details—the bell, the slate, the original floor, the classic gable roof—the sound of children still seems to echo throughout the building.

The slant of the gable roof and the charm of the original wide-plank pine floors are among the features that make this building special, left. They, most of all, bring forth its schoolhouse spirit. Vallone added the oak beam and round window above the door to give a perception of the space that would make it seem more comfortable.

The sleekness of slate on the kitchen countertop, right, lends a contemporary air while harking back to the original schoolhouse blackboards. The tall chairs are framed in the same black steel used for the ladder to the loft. The contrast of old and new is apparent where the chairs reach the knotted pine floors below.

Country spirit is apparent in the design of the home, left and above. Even so, there are contrasts everywhere that lend interest and keep the schoolhouse from resembling a museum. An old wooden sled hangs below careful track lighting, and an antique country dining table faces a sliding glass door.

Gatehouse, *Wells-next-the-Sea, England*

When architect Nicholas Hills gets to his home just outside Wells-next-the-Sea, he stops at the gate, and stays there. For this entryway is his home—a converted gatehouse that welcomed visitors to the eighteenth-century estate within. Named Holkham Hall, the estate was designed in the 1730s by William Kent. The arched entryway was built at the same time as a dramatic and impressive introduction to the massive house and grounds. After the northern entrance to the estate became more frequently used than this southern entrance, the gatehouse was used as a hunting lodge.

It became a home after Nicholas Hills found it while on vacation twenty years ago in Wells-next-the-Sea and made an agreement with the tenant of the estate to rent it. Moving into an arch has its difficulties: The building was in derelict condition after sitting empty for over fifty years, and the stairs and middle floor of the right wing were gone. So were most of the windows, which had been boarded up against the elements. At some point, the chimneys had been sealed and a roof had been placed over their openings. There had never been any water or electricity in the building.

Hills had water piped in from the cattle trough that sits inside the gate, but the building is so remotely located that he still has no electricity. He says that chopping wood for the fireplaces and using oil lamps and candles make him feel like he's living in the time the gatehouse was built.

The arched gateway to Holkham Hall, opposite page, is a grand entrance—and home to architect Nicholas Hills. The rounded window in the main room above the arch, above, offers a dramatic view of the stretching road and countryside.

He has built two small guest rooms in the right wing, which he calls the "Stranger's Wing," and has put the kitchen and dining areas in the left wing. While these areas are charming, the real reason to live in an arch can be found in the dramatic space spanning it: The light room above the curve of this building is the reward of being there. A stone staircase winds up from below and opens out into the huge room. Here the original lunette window lets in a view of the surrounding countryside from above the other rooms, and the entry road that splits it lies straight ahead like an invitation, but ends in some trees in the distance, creating an effect of mystery. The marvelous brick and wood-beamed room serves as a living area during the day, and a sofa that directly echoes the shape of the window turns into a bed at night. The obelisk bookshelves in this room reflect the stone obelisk just up the drive that was also designed by William Kent.

The design of the rest of the house also reinforces the history and architecture of the arch. Hill painted trompe l'oeil stone on the wood cabinets in the kitchen "to try and keep an echo of the eighteenth century," he says. Mounted deer heads recall the former hunting life of the building. And Kent's original plans for the arch, hand-tinted by Hill, hang on the wall.

The character of the arch, though, can be found as much in what is *around* as what is within it. Because of its original function, the building sits alone in the solitary countryside. And getting to it is just as rural an experience: "Follow the narrow lane through the trees until you come to the spot where five roads converge, cross them bearing right and there it is." The estate is still maintained and farmed by a descendant of the original owners. There is green everywhere, and on either side of the drive is a majestic avenue of oak trees, which grew, legend has it, from acorns that were used to pack sculptures sent from Italy centuries ago. Sheep graze below the trees, and cows can be seen outside Hills's door.

There are certainly some eccentricities that come with living in such a place. Hills get his mail through the bathroom window, where the postman drops it on his way to the main house. The cows have broken much of his garden furniture and trampled his flowerpots. He believes this is all part of the rustic charm of living in his gatehouse: "I have permission to fence this off and keep the cattle out, but on the other hand, there is something delicious about living in a field."

In the main room above the arch, opposite page, light streams in through the oversized windows. The antlers above them are a reminder of the building's past life as a hunting lodge. The arched door, above, is an echo of the building itself.

The vast space in a ballroom is scaled down to human proportions with the help of a trellised "catwalk" that runs around the building and two walls that define the living area, opposite page. The big, two-story living area opens out onto smaller rooms at both levels, as the plans show, far right. Across from the enclosed space sits the dining area, right, where a three-dimensional work by Frank Stella heightens the drama of the space.

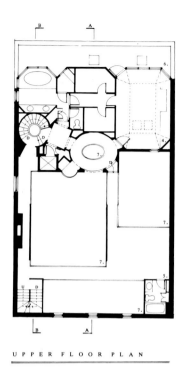

UPPER FLOOR PLAN

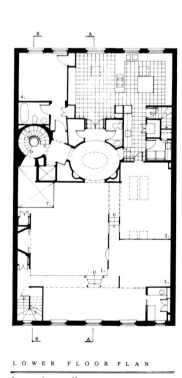

LOWER FLOOR PLAN

0   8   12

1. LIVING ROOM
2. DINING ROOM
3. LIBRARY
4. BEDROOM
5. LOFT
6. TERRACE
7. OPEN TO BELOW

Ballroom, *Boston, MA*

Visitors may still get the urge to dance in the ballroom that architect Graham Gund turned into a home for a Boston couple. The vast expanse of wood floor in the living area could still be glided across, and although the space has been transformed into something new and certainly contemporary, its monumentality and sense of drama remain.

The ballroom was constructed in 1905 in the upper half of a building whose lower floors housed servants' quarters and a garage. This kind of detached "wing" was not unusual in turn-of-the-century Boston: A single wealthy family would own the building to provide space for all their needs outside the main house. The plain brick structure sits on historic Beacon Hill in a former alley—a quiet block-long street that nevertheless is not far from the bustle of the city center.

Most of what Gund saw when he first walked into the ballroom was raw space—soaring ceilings two stories high and a forty-by-forty-foot floor. But the room, which was designed to be lit up only at night, was dark and dreary during the day; double-hung windows at the front of the building were the only source of natural light. And though it was grand, it was relatively straightforward: an English Baronial-style room with a fake wood-beam ceiling, simple plaster walls, wood floors, plain wrought-iron chandeliers, and an over-scaled fireplace. Not much of this was appropriate for a home. So

The piano presides on the other side of the living room, past the white columns, and among an expanse of polished floors, right. The careful placement of architecture and objects in areas such as these creates quite an effect. As one resident says, "We don't have a panoramic view outside—just the narrow street—so we had to create our views inside the home."

Gund opened up the dark dropped ceilings to let in more light and volume. The original walls and floors were in disrepair and had to be replastered and relaid. And the chandeliers, though charmingly anachronistic, would not fit into any design scheme for a contemporary home. Only the large fireplace was saved.

Gund's main challenge was to make the huge space comfortable for living by breaking it into smaller areas, while keeping the open spirit of the original ballroom. Instead of installing a full ceiling between the two stories, he kept the whole central space open, tucking rooms into the corners and sides of the building that are all accessible from a new "catwalk" running around the second-story level. The maple handrails of the catwalk are designed like trellises so that everything is visible through them. Then to scale down the volume for confortable living, Gund designed a little area set off within the larger one that holds the living room. This partial enclosure is made from two huge curving contemporary walls on either side—maple panels inlaid with ebony in a pattern that echoes the grid of the trellises. The outdoor feeling of the trellises, the openings in the walls that resemble doors and windows, and the balconies along the catwalks all bring to mind a courtyard, evoking the same feeling of intimacy and protection within the great space that a real courtyard does in the outdoors.

The other priority of the conversion was lightening up the space, which Gund achieved with a series of porthole windows at the front of the building and skylights in darker areas such as the entry hall. The light shines in gridded patterns on the floor of the main room through the panels of the big original double-hung windows in the front, which are picked up by the gridded designs in the rest of the home. Gund also used light-colored materials throughout—off-white and pale finishes, maple for flooring and the trim of architectural elements. The result is a surprisingly bright space where, as the owners say, "the light really dances." And it seems even brighter in contrast with the dark brick closeness of the nineteenth-century street it sits on.

Standing on a balcony overlooking the space, the residents can survey its past and present grandeur. The sweep of space, the stature of the new white columns bordering the steps leading into the living room, the grand piano sitting alone on expanses of wood floor evoke the particular sense of celebration and suspense that only a ballroom can. One can almost imagine the orchestra playing below, and the couples swirling in time.

In what was once an alley lined with stables, garages, and servants quarters, sits this structure, above. The upper two stories of the building once held the ballroom; they are now a light-filled residence due to the original double-hung windows and architect Graham Gund's porthole additions. "The light really dances here," says one of the residents.

The "house within a house" created by the freestanding walls and "catwalk" gives a comforting sense of enclosure, right; even when it goes behind the walls, the "catwalk" runs continuously around the space. The big brass doors in one wall cover the massive original fireplace when not in use.

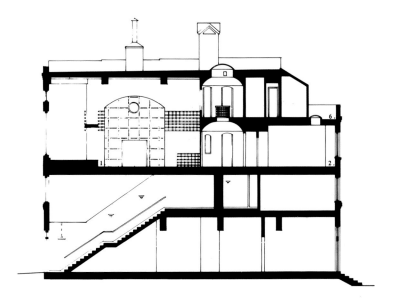

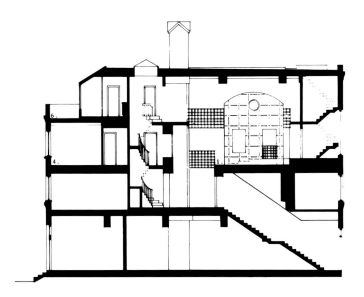

Drawings show a cross section of the ballroom from the side. The side facing the dining room, above left, holds the elevators, while the side facing the entryway, lower left, holds the stairs. Only the top two floors of the building were the ballroom; the bottom floors held a garage and servants quarters that were converted into another residence.

Pigsty, *Peschici, Italy*

A pigsty may seem a singularly unlikely structure to convert, but this country home in Peschici, Italy, was transformed from what was a relatively significant little building in the life of a remote rural village. For just twenty years ago, the pigs were Peschici's street cleaners and occupied a position of some importance. In the intervening years, the village invested in street-cleaning machines, and the building is now happily inhabited by people.

In fact, the former pigsty, with its original storybook doors and windows, is only part of the two-story home. The second story has a past of its own: It was built into the old fortification wall of the town as a residence long before the present owners, a couple from England, took over both it and the pigsty and connected the two with an interior stairway. Although they moved into the very walls of the city, the couple received less than a warm welcome at first, as the townspeople were not used to strangers. But the new residents have found their place there—a bright, cleanly designed one that hints of pigs only in the most charming ways.

A second-floor balcony was added to the outside of the fortification, but the rest of the exterior was cleaned up and left much the same as when pigs and an occasional donkey called it home.

More substantive changes were made inside, but the plans for them were not easily communicated. Although the owners speak Italian, the particular dialect of the village was way beyond their

Arches are a dominant theme on the second level, right, which was built into the fortification wall of the town. The table is a traditional piece painted bright blue for contemporary expression, and the chairs that sit at it are actually pews that were rescued from the church across the street and cut up.

understanding, so the local architect had to convey his thoughts to them in sketches. These were transformed into a design that really works for the house, but the owners weren't sure of that at the time. What they got, however, was worth their trust: a curious staircase, narrow and winding, built into the thick walls to connect the upper and lower floors; a new bedroom and bath whose lines join with the original ones to bring out the best in the pigsty; and an evocative sense of the country roots of the place.

Although the architect capitalized on the cozy, cavelike atmosphere of the original building, the space manages not to seem closed. Both upstairs and down, the ceilings are low and the walls eccentric, since the pigs did not need much height, and the rooms built into the fortification wall needed to be arched for support. So white paint was used throughout to open up the space and give it a bright, clean look. Local red tiling covers much of the surface area—walls, floors, countertops—and brings out the country spirit of the structure.

Many of the interior elements have an almost organic feel: the winding staircase that continues the intimacy of the original structure so well that it is hard to believe the stairs were not always there; the bedroom and bath carved into the low, curving walls of the former pigsty; the shower built into a meeting of sculptured, undulating walls that remind one how special the structure is. The four-by-six-foot mangers that once fed the pigs were completely covered in tile, and now support the bed and bathroom basin. There is even a trap door in the second-story floor that was once used to throw food down to the animals, kept as a reminder of the building's origins.

The furnishings reflect not only the building's history, but its environment as well. The dining room chairs were cut from pews rescued from the church across the way—in fact, the priest traded the centuries-old treasures, some of them praying benches with kneeling posts on the back, for plastic chairs the owners were happy to part with. And there are indications throughout of the village's local industry—a fisherman's lamp in the kitchen, lobster traps hanging from the ceiling as decoration.

This is a country cottage with a difference: Its former occupants not only give it a unique history but a special charm as well. And its new owners have retained its character so well that it is the perfect embodiment of the rough honesty of a rural village lost somewhere in Italy.

A shower was placed in the meeting of sculptured walls, above. Like much of the rest of this building, the rooms here are lined in red tile. Elsewhere in the bathroom, the mangers where the pigs fed were covered with the same tile, and the sinks were placed on top.

The new stone spiral staircase winds down from the second level to the pigsty, above, fitting in so closely both physically and in terms of design that it seems as though it has always been there. Beds in the former pigsty sit on the mangers that have been tiled over, right. The kitchen is a study in red tile, opposite page, reflecting the rusticity of the building.

The back view of this former garage, opposite page, is a portrait in light. No draperies were used in the home, so light always comes right through the marvelous windows. The windows in the kitchen, above, resemble small garage doors.

Garage, *Nashville, TN*

The temptation on driving up to the Armistead home in Nashville is to keep on going, right into the building. For the home is a former garage and, charmingly, still looks like one. A garage may seem a mundane starting point for a conversion, bringing to mind concrete, white parking lines, and exhaust. Not every garage, however, is built in Elizabethan Tudor style, or listed on the National Register of Historic Places. This one is special. Its architecture is distinctive because it speaks not only of another use but of another day as well. It was built in 1915 for the Belle Meade apartments, a gracious piece of Tudor-style history that sits in a residential section of Nashville, and its exterior matches that of the buildings that surround it.

The straightforward, practical personality of a garage—even as distinguished a garage as this—seemed like the perfect answer to the owners' wish to "simplify and unclutter" their lives. Mrs. Armistead grew up in the apartment buildings, which have belonged to her family almost since they were built, and she liked the idea of doing something new to a place so old.

Architect Bryant Glasgow and architectural designer Sharon Pigott came in to restore as much as to convert, for the historical registry had very specific guidelines about what could and, more often, could not be done to the building. Their basic requirement was that the public views, such as the front exterior, look as they did when the structure was built, leaving the more private areas for contemporary expression and innovation.

The building had been abandoned for some time and was in severe disrepair—water leaked through falling plaster, and daylight streamed through holes in the roof. The second floor had

been the servants' quarters, so it was designed to be habitable and was therefore easier to convert, but the garage below had uneven slabs of concrete for floors and large, beautiful—but dilapidated—doors for walls. The entire building lacked insulation and heating and cooling systems.

The first step was to clear out the garage, which was filled with junk and some more valuable items—such as Rolls-Royces that were stored there and never used. Low beams had to be removed to open up the space.

The architects' basic approach struck a balance between the building's historic qualities and the owners' contemporary tastes by keeping the exterior ordered and traditional and making the interior a contemporary place, open and filled with light. The ma-terials were an important part of integrating the old and the new. The idea was, as Glasgow says, to "put back materials that resem-bled what had been there before, but in a way that would bring the building up to date." That meant using wood, brick, and lots of glass. The wonderfully patterned doors were replaced with whole fixed walls of windows that were designed in the same pan-eled configurations as the old doors. So the facade of the building looks much as it always has, respecting the demands of the registry and the ethics of historic preservation. And the windows fill the home with light, as well as retain the spirit of the garage. Even the windows on the sides of the building, which do not directly

imitate the doors, take cues from them—in the kitchen, they cover only the top half of the wall but consist of sectioned panels of glass that make them look like small garage doors.

The new roofing material is an approximation of the old, and matches the grand Tudor roofs of the Belle Meade apartments. The only major change to the exterior was made in the back, where a second-floor balcony supported by columns opens up the master bedroom and gives a strong regional air to the Southern house. A long line of French doors, rather than garage doors, opens out into the garden; they are also in the same style as the original doors.

Inside there is light, whiteness, and an order and straightfor-ward symmetry that parallels the linear "garage door" windows and falls in line with the overall simple character of the structure. New beechwood floors were laid on top of the old concrete, and a contemporary stairway of slatted wood, descending from the for-mer servants' quarters to the garage, continues the clean, evenly patterned lines of the space. Light, neutral walls, and pickled flooring further a feeling of spaciousness, and contemporary art and native crafts mix with the antiques to extend the sense of old and new living together.

The Rolls-Royces have lost their home, but the Armisteads have found one, and it is eminently more comfortable and livable than anyone would expect of an old garage.

The interior of this home is dominated by the wall of windows, above, which copy the design of the original garage doors. The clean, evenly paced patterns of the windows are carried through in the interior design, where glass and light colors are used to keep the space clean and uncluttered.

Because of the building's age and architectural distinctiveness, the National Register required the front, opposite page, to remain basically unchanged. It still looks very much like a garage. The tree-shaded lot is perfect for southern living. The interior design continues the southern flair, right.

Stone Church, *Hillsboro, VA*

Aside from the people who knock on the door of Connie and Lawrence Ormes's converted church asking to see the pastor, the simple stone structure has been a uniquely peaceful place to live. The church, on Virginia farm land in the foothills of the Blue Ridge mountains, is typical of the public buildings raised by little communities in those days—small, serviceable, and simply built to meet the needs of citizens. More than that—a spire, for instance—was beyond the community's resources.

The church's history is less peaceful than its spirit: Built in 1833 by the Methodist Episcopals, it later broke from the Episcopalians to be a Methodist church. During the Civil War, parishioners from the North and the South worshipped here separately. It was served mostly by a circuit pastor who rode on horseback between the various churches, preaching when he was there and relying on the people of the congregation to fill in the rest of the time. The little one-room building then became a meeting area for the com-

munity until 1959. It sat empty for almost a decade until Lawrence Ormes's parents bought it and converted it into what was intended to be a place for retirement, but instead it was simply rented out for the next several years.

Now the Ormeses have taken it over—having bought it from his parents—and created yet another life for the building, this time as a family home. The family needed more room, so they added on to the building in a way that was sensible for meeting their needs yet sensitive to the structure, carefully complementing its materials and spirit. They added a new wing and filled it with bedrooms for the large family. To avoid interfering with a 200-year-old oak tree in the front, the wing was not attached to the original structure, but to the left of the parents' earlier addition, which stretches straight back to the rear of the church. It continues the beautiful traditional stonework of the original building. The fieldstones came from the surrounding property, as they had 150 years earlier,

and a stonemason matched the mortar almost exactly, experimenting with sand from different areas to get the same color, consistency, and texture. Stained beaded cedar siding was used for the area just below the roof to blend in with both the rustic stone and the surrounding woods.

Inside, the original gable-roofed structure holds the living and dining areas, and up the beautiful 150-year-old winding stairway is the old slave loft from much earlier days, now made into a bedroom and bathroom. The stonework on the floor of the main room was installed during the first conversion, as the random-width pine, oak, and walnut church floor had been partially eaten by termites and had to be taken up in any case to accommodate the plumbing and electrical lines that the building lacked. Nevertheless, some of the original floor was salvaged, treated, and used for the kitchen floor in the earlier addition.

The kitchen, reached by a doorway at the back of the church, is in complete character with the old building. What was once part of the church's stone exterior is now the kitchen's inner wall. And in keeping with the rustic feeling of the house, the cabinets were constructed of pine taken from the boards of an old northern Virginia barn. Even the water that flows through the taps has its source in the Virginia woods—in this case, a lovely spring behind the old church that was previously the site of community picnics.

Beyond the wavy, hand-blown glass of the original windows in the dining room is the old churchyard, dating back almost to the founding of the church. Connie Ormes has a relaxed attitude about living with a cemetery in her backyard: "These are the quietest neighbors I've ever had. If I have guests for dinner who are really bothered by tombstones, I seat them with their backs to the window." Indeed, the cemetery only enriches the vivid sense of history that surrounds the building. Visitors stop by to see the graves of local heroes and renegades, or to trace their genealogy. The Ormeses' property is descended on yearly by the Daughters of the Confederacy, who come to put a flag on the grave of an infamous local assassinated at Harper's Ferry.

The fact that Lawrence Ormes grew up on the adjoining farm makes the circle of history complete, and the sense of continuity, endurance, and serenity that pervades this conversion is reflected in the very name of the church: "Salem," an old form of the word "Jerusalem," meaning city of peace. "This," Connie Ormes says, "is *our* city of peace."

The original windows looking out onto the graveyard, opposite page and below, are so old one can see the waves in the hand-blown glass. There is history in the graveyard, too, and people from the area still come to see it and the building where they attended church as children.

Power Station, *Dallas, TX*

In a city like Dallas, where the word "old" is used pejoratively, it is somewhat remarkable that a 1920s electrical substation should be turned into a home. Of course, it would be remarkable anywhere, and architect Gary Cunningham's treatment of the conversion for a high-profile couple makes it all the more striking. The project does fit a word used positively in Dallas: "big." Everything about the home is big—the massive brick and limestone-detailed exterior; the building's 6,000 square feet broken into three floors; the twenty-ton crane that was used to lift electrical equipment and now hangs right outside the dining room. And, true to its roots, the house is powerful. Cunningham has charged the place with energy, literally exposing its electricity and inner workings. Trenches where wiring runs were left in place and glassed over; electrical lines can be seen passing through here and there; and the connections, colors, and complexity of the electrical process are everywhere in evidence.

The North Dallas Power and Light Substation was one of five identical buildings that took power from the main plant downtown and broke it up into different levels for various uses, whether for homes, businesses, streetcars, or street lights. Because the substation took masses of raw power and refined them for so many uses it was intricate and multi-layered—there were electrical rivers and routes that traveled to different places to produce different types of power. And as Cunningham says, "It was not as simple as just power in and power out; there were steps up, down, and sideways, changing color as they went." His conversion certainly reflects the complexity of the building's original use.

After it "brought progress to Dallas," as an old ad proclaimed, the building was taken out of commission in the 1960s. There was a tremendous amount of waste in it when the conversion began.

The third-floor ballroom of the converted power station, opposite page, has sources of light from both above and below, created by old elements in the building. Architect Gary Cunningham installed glass in the ceiling in place of old louvers, which acted as air-exhaust vents, to create industrial skylights. Glass was also used to fill the holes in the floor created when the old conduit boxes were torn out. The ceiling of original trusses and floors of new maple wood are well worth illuminating. The building before conversion, above, was so full of debris that it took five months to clean it out.

Cunningham intended to formulate the design of the building while it was being cleaned up, but what was uncovered during that process ended up determining the design. "What began as a cleanup," Cunningham says, "became an archaeological dig." Strange electrical chaseways and porcelain isolators were discovered beneath layers of pigeon dung; interior columns of raw steel were sandblasted, revealing an amazing burnished color; brick walls were cleaned, uncovering a warmth surprising in such an industrial structure. It was at this point that Cunningham and his clients agreed that everything in the building should be exposed, saved, and shown.

The design became an ongoing process, decided as new properties of the building were discovered. The exterior was cleaned, and the structure of the building was left pretty much alone. Stairs and windows are all original. And the high brick walls, fence, and huge masonry enclosure that once served to muffle noise coming from the power station now provide security and block sound coming the other way—from the mixed residential and commercial neighborhood in which the building sits. Inside, the building looks like a museum of electricity, starting right at the front door, where a glass awning shows off a series of electrical power lines extending from a power pole. From here, these lines of power, which currently serve the house, can be traced the length of the building through a glass shaft. Ironically, the building had no incoming power because it made its own, so the new power for the house was placed in an existing raceway, which ends in a series of intriguing switches. A glassed-over trough runs under the dining room table, containing copper-clad electrical lines backlit by fiber optics. Overhead are exposed conduits and dozens of lights that have been placed in electrical isolators.

New plumbing and wiring, too, remain exposed. Even the process of conversion has been left on display, layering the original history of the building with recent history. When a door had to be punched through a wall or workers had to tear into a piece of concrete, the broken bricks and jagged edges were left as they were and glazed with a clear finish. With all this exposed construction, Cunningham was faced with unusual architectural decisions. "Because everything was so visible," he says, "every detail was up for

Lit up at night, the power station, above, still looks like a dramatic source of electricity. While it is startling to find chairs and tables among the industrial and electrical components running through the building, opposite page, there actually is plenty of space devoted to living here. In addition to the parlor, kitchen, and dining room, the "urban mansion" contains three bedrooms, a library, a small gallery for art, a ballroom, several sitting areas, a butler's pantry and utility room off the kitchen, a wine cellar, and a bowling lawn and sculpture garden on the roof featuring works made from pieces found in the building. There is a separate workspace in the garage.

A crane hangs just out-
side the dining room,
right. Although the twen-
ty-ton crane was originally
used to hoist electrical
equipment, it came in
handy during the conver-
sion. The stairs rise up
from here, bounded by
sheets of wire-reinforced
glass that have been ag-
gressively bolted to the
steel pipe railing. A view
of the building from the
roof, opposite page,
shows its practical industrial stature.

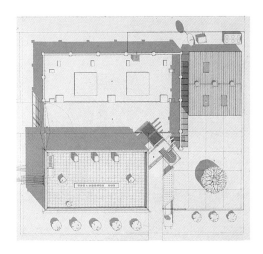

discussion and had to be understood—how wire was run, how pipe was put in, how that pipe turned, how a plumber made a joint." He took advantage of these exposed elements to take symbolic risks, crossing the defunct electrical wiring with the new plumbing fixtures. This visual cross of electricity and water provokes much excitement, because it is, as Cunningham says, "dangerous emotionally."

When the maze of concrete and stone conduit boxes was jack-hammered and taken out of the first floor, a series of large slots was left in the ceiling—and in the second-story floor. Rather than fill them in, Cunningham installed glass panels, which filter in natural light during the daytime and are lit from below at night, creating a sense of continuous space. Any elements that couldn't be left in place were used elsewhere. The steel beams cut out to make room for the elevator, for example, were made into seats for the roof garden.

New materials are industrial rather than residential. A new topping of concrete was laid on the first floor; doors, storage closets, and stair treads were made from industrial-grade fir; and the stair rails were assembled from steel pipe and connectors. And just to make sure that this idea was taken all the way, Cunningham installed a powder room of sandblasted glass and a masonry coat closet. The elevator was stripped and encased in glass to show off its inside mechanisms; when it reaches the third floor it meets a concrete pavilion that once held explosive batteries and now contains a bathroom.

In direct contrast to the industrial design, the layout of the house was based on Texas mansions of the 1920s. So there is a parlor off the stairs on the first floor, and the dining room, kitchen, and library are just beyond. The second floor holds three bedrooms, leaving the third for a grand ballroom.

For Cunningham, both the joy and the challenge of the project derive from its complexity, its layering of old and new, the fact that "there was a history there and a lot of ghosts." The building, he says, "isn't glorious like a church, and it isn't a great historical building, but it had the very important purpose of bringing electricity to a city." That purpose—and the spirit, integrity, and logic of the building—is never forgotten in this unique conversion.

The red brick building with neoclassical limestone details is a classic industrial structure, right. The owners say that they were happy "to let the building be itself," which meant saving as many of its components as possible. Pieces found during cleanup were stockpiled and used for other purposes; during what became a simultaneous process of design, demolition, and construction, no original element nor its use was ignored.

Limestone-aggregate concrete block boxes were newly built as separate pavilions, left and above, for the more private functions of living, leaving the shell of the building untouched while creating living spaces on a more intimate scale. The boxes are only eight feet tall so as not to interrupt the flow of space, but are glazed with glass to the thirteen-and-a-half-foot ceiling above for acoustical privacy.

The sawmill by the Silvermine River dramatically hovers over the water, opposite page. After all these years, the site and the building have become interwoven; a large sycamore tree grows right through the second story deck. The river flows past the new sitting room, above, where many windows make one striking view.

Sawmill, *Connecticut*

Most residents of converted buildings live with a history, but Evan and Mary Vann Hunter live with many. Their home on the Silvermine River in Connecticut was originally a sawmill built in the 1770s, but it has since been a cotton-batting mill, a doorknob factory, a spindle mill, a landscape artist's studio, and a home to others, most recently an artist and his wife. The Hunters have continued what seems to have become a tradition of creativity in the house. Evan Hunter is the famed writer of mystery novels (and, under the pseudonym Ed McBain, police stories), and Mary Vann is a novelist. The house is a layering of many lives, with charming and distinct contributions from them and from the building's various uses.

What is most striking about the home is the spirit of the mill, retained throughout in original elements: the curious, low-ceilinged rooms; the exposed beams of ancient wood (some of which bear carved Roman numerals, so that the builders would place them correctly); and the old shaft and turbine, which can just be made out by peering into the damp darkness behind a door underneath the building. The old floors slant charmingly from age, so furniture is propped up on one side with shims; as Mary Vann explains, "You just have to do things like that in this house."

The building was first converted into a studio and home by landscape painter Frank Townsend Hutchens in 1912. A 1914 issue of *Suburban Life Magazine*, in which the story of that early

The post-and-beam structure of the mill is evident in the living room, opposite page, where original beams and columns dominate. A new expanse of glass was installed here for a first-floor view of the river. This plan of the home, right, shows the street side of the building, with the placement of the original turbine room underneath. The house made its own electricity until 1910.

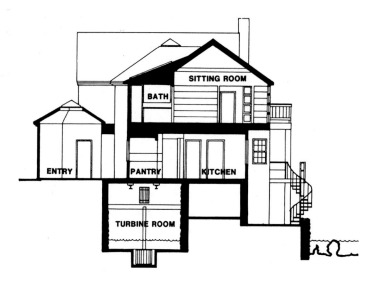

conversion is told, says that Hutchens found the place "not only a haven of refuge but a constant inspiration." It was probably the river flowing by and the surrounding trees of which he was speaking, the fact that the old mill sits practically *in* the water and almost becomes a part of the woods.

The wood floors Hutchens had installed throughout the main part of the house are still there, as are the other elements that made it homelike—intimate rooms, a fireplace, a nineteenth-century door frame that he brought down from Maine. But his most evocative contributions are the cast-iron balconies. Neither mill-like nor New England in character, they come as a delightful surprise every time one looks at the building. Hutchens brought the balconies from New Orleans but did not leave an explanation of the legend on them that says simply, "W. W. Storey, 1861."

There are signs of other lives throughout. When part of the siding was taken off during the Hunters' own renovation, the old red-painted wood that was the original mill siding was discovered underneath with names and dates carved in it. A chiseled stone reading "Mabel's Rock Garden, 1932" was found near the garage where Mabel, whoever she was, must have tended her garden, as was a brass bird that was probably molded in the kiln down the river by an artist who worked at the mill (today only the lines of the kiln's foundation are left). And the rustic wood-lined kitchen, a study in craftsmanship, was left by the most recent artist resident and his wife, as were his wonderful drawings of the mill house. There was even history to be found in the ground; when the old foundation was dug up to make alterations, broken shards of pottery and an old pipe without a stem from the building's mill days were uncovered.

Now the Hunters have added their contributions to the building—theirs and Richard Bergmann's, the architect who altered the house for them and enlarged it by 30 percent. The couple's main

consideration was how to close off the house from the road on one side and open it up to the river on the other. Because it was built as a mill, views were not taken into consideration: From nowhere within could one see the river flowing just outside. In addition, the house, on just 1.3 acres of land, sits very close to the road and there is nothing to buffer the noise and provide privacy. Finally, after the building's many incarnations, no one really knew where the front door had been—and few guests could find the present one, tucked awkwardly on the side of the house.

To solve the problems—and add some much-needed room—Bergmann built three additions. The first is an entryway, complete with the little windows that he used throughout to recall the mill's original factory-like windows. Bergmann extended it from the old entryway, and the door was moved so that it was more accessible. Onto the living room he added a den, which is faced on the outside with a six-foot-high stone wall. The stone is in keeping with the spirit of the building and makes the road seem far away. Above the wall is a thirty-foot skylight that generously lets light into the dark building.

The Hunters' major addition was the sitting room upstairs that overlooks the river through dozens of two-by-two-foot windows. Once an outdoor balcony, the sitting room now provides fifty little views of the waterfall that add up to a dramatic composite. Bergmann used smaller windows instead of a big expanse of glass because, he says, "If you stand next to floor-to-ceiling glass with water rushing by you, you can feel unprotected. Besides, there is the notion of framing smaller views rather than open panoramas."

To support the addition from below, Bergmann used telephone poles, rough-hewn enough to look natural with the mill. Other changes included the creation of a master bedroom from two small rooms that overlook the river, staining the cedar-shingled exterior dark brown in the spirit of mill colors, and generally updating the building from a state of disrepair.

Although the entrance side of the house faces the road so closely that it makes one feel as though the world is going by, remarkably there is another world just a few yards through the house where the building nearly meets the water. Here one can hear the constant rush of the river and feel the power that drove the mill, but also the tranquility of the flowing water. As Mary Vann says, "We are close to everything in one way, but I can really get kind of lost here in the woods."

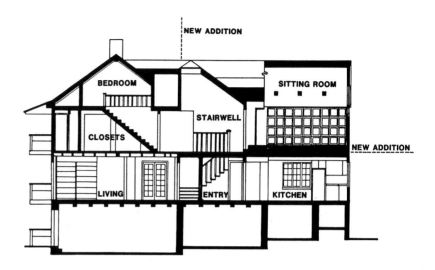

New wood beams echo the old in the sitting room, opposite page. The side of the house facing the river is detailed in the plan, above. One of the joys of living in such a building, owner Mary Vann Hunter says, is that "you find little surprises, evidence of past lives that give the home texture and significance."

Fifty little windows in the new sitting room at the back of the home look out onto the Silvermine River, above. A photograph of the building taken before the conversion, right, shows the confusing placement of the front door and the run-down state of the structure.

The little windows are repeated in the new entryway where, with the help of a skylight, they usher light into what previously was a dark building, left. The windows recall the originals of the mill, and the skylight brings in a sense of the contemporary. Skylights and fans are found throughout the home, as they are in many converted buildings.

The converted commercial building near Dupont Circle in Washington, D.C., above, offers an unusual arrangement of residential space. The space is vertical rather than horizontal, so the rooms are taller than they are wide, and the important measure is in cubic feet rather than square feet. In the entry hall, opposite page, are the first of the paneless windows that occur throughout the house. They help to counter the perception of vertical space in the building.

Commercial Building, *Washington, D.C.*

Architect Mark McInturff's conversion of a commercial building in Washington, D.C., is a study in light and drama. When the shop on the ground floor of the building—most recently selling futons—closed, the couple who inhabited the upper floor asked McInturff to help them expand downward. He responded with striking sculptural elements such as a curved staircase, new light sources like the skylight that tops the building—and a regard for the straightforward nature of the original structure.

What McInturff had to work with was a plain turn-of-the-century storefront, typical of many from the era and recalling the small-town quality that once characterized much of Washington. He wanted to honor that lack of pretension by keeping the inside elemental—clean but not overly clever, interesting but informal. The structure was small and slightly eccentric—at least for a home, since most of the space is vertical—and it needed light and order to make it livable. So, listening to the owners' request for a "loft-like" home, McInturff kept to plain wood floors and white walls, open spaces and natural light to fill them. The basic design has what the architect refers to as a "Shaker simplicity," but his solutions to architectural problems, achieved with the introduction of new elements, add interest and definition to the space.

The shell of the building was about all that could be retained; most of the interior elements, including doors, windows, nearly all the flooring, and the plumbing and electricity, are new. McInturff's stairway connecting the first and second floors became the

central—and most exciting—element of the home. It winds up, opening into an impressive vertical space and a skylight above. A tower-like balcony at the top of the stairs provides a lookout to the interior landscape.

Here on the second story, which holds the dining room, the light comes in from everywhere—from the skylight that sits right above the tower and echoes its circular shape, from the new windows whose patterns echo those of the shop windows below. It floods down to the first floor, opening up the small space.

In the entry hall there is another carryover from the original building—high ceilings that recall the stores of yesterday that stretched up with rows of merchandise. Glass in neat patterns by the door of the entry hall brings to mind shop windows, but here they have been sandblasted for privacy.

It is the pane-less interior windows, however, that really affect the perception of space. They start in the entry hall and recur throughout the house: in the tower at the top of the stair, stretching down the line of the hallway and into the living room on the first floor. The windows, McInturff says, "keep the eye guessing," making the small space seem larger.

The mind is kept guessing, too. On the one hand, the windows suggest separate rooms by visually enclosing discrete areas of space. But on the other, they are open and look out onto the other "rooms," and there is the reality of the flow of these spaces with no walls between them—the entry hall extends upward to the dining room, for instance, but it also extends outward to the living room on the same story. So there is separation and continuity at the same time, allowing the *idea* of many rooms but the reality of one big open one, and expanding the home in a way that few other solutions would do.

The series of interior windows that extend from the entryway into the living room are skewered together with a long continuous light fixture—"like a shish kebab," McInturff says—to provide a rigorous order for the small space and also to unify it, again, even as the windows themselves divide it up.

The project was completed for only $50,000, but the decision to stick to basics was philosophical as well as budgetary. In a conversion whose keynote was simplicity, McInturff found elements that created interest while remaining simple: light, layering, and a sense of drama that has won many awards for the little house next to the shoe shop.

Over 3,200 cubic feet are contained in the narrow building, above. The ceilings on each floor are twelve feet high. In this home an "upside down" plan was carried out, which places the more public areas such as the dining room, opposite page, on the upper floor to capture light and views not available on the lower story.

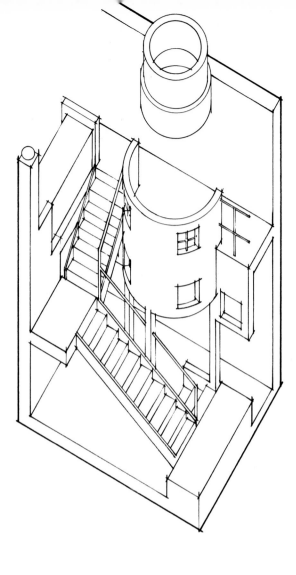

The prominence of the staircase in the design of the building is evident in the drawing, above, which depicts the rounded bannister at the top of the stair and the skylight, which echoes it. The circular form of the balcony shoots all the way through the building, from the entryway, right, where its curve begins overhead, to the second floor, opposite page, where it forms a lookout point.

The tower of St. Alban, left, sits in the center of the street as well as in the center of London. The tower was all that was left of the church after a night raid in World War II. Inside, opposite page, the look is formal. The walls of the blue bedroom on the fourth floor, however, were covered with paint and crayon in an unconventional treatment.

Bell Tower, *London, England*

When the residents of a converted bell tower in London refer to their home as being in the center of the city, they are speaking of a place that literally sits in the middle of a street running through the oldest settled area in London. Looking like a drawing taken from an architectural textbook and placed on the street, the tower sits all alone yet in the middle of everything. It splits the street so that traffic flows on all sides at its base, and the buildings that make up the financial district of London surround it.

But it is not only the tower's location that is central to London— its history is, too. It is built on the site of the first Roman garrison fort, which later became the location for the Saxon royal palace. In the eighth century, the King dedicated a chapel there to St. Alban, the first English martyr. When that building began to fall apart, it was replaced by another that was later destroyed in the Great Fire of London in 1666. In 1682 Sir Christopher Wren, although he was in the throes of reconstructing St. Paul's Cathedral, agreed to design a new church and bell tower for the site.

The Gothic architecture of the church and tower was a true departure for Wren, but he used it to honor the remarkable past of the site. The tower stands seventy-two feet tall and contains 976 square feet within. Its walls are five feet thick at the base and diminish as the tower rises.

The church was tragically leveled during a night raid in the Second World War, and the bell tower is all that remained. Today, the Tower of St. Alban stands as a Gothic monument to a long and lively history.

Not many offices have floor-to-ceiling windows, much less church windows designed by Sir Christopher Wren. The leaded-glass windows are on all sides of the tower, which, because of its site, means there are views from all four sides.

In converting the building recently for an American family, Frederick Smith Burns, the architect, had to work with a magnificent-looking piece of architecture of little functional value. When he took it on, the tower was falling into dereliction. And its particular structure did not make its conversion into a residence any easier. As home only to a bell, the tower, of course, did not have any need for—nor did it contain—a roof, any floors, or evenly placed windows.

Construction was a challenge. The extreme narrowness of the tower meant that its six floors had to be inserted from above. "We put on a roof and worked downwards," says Burns matter-of-factly. As if the structure of the building were not enough to work around, its history asserted itself in the middle of the project, temporarily halting work: Human bones were found under the ground floor, and the Museum of London carried out an archeological dig before work was resumed.

There is one room to each floor of the tower. Each is about fourteen feet square, but because the walls get thinner as the tower gets higher, every successive floor is slightly larger than the one below it. The building has a shoulder-width stone staircase spiraling up to connect the floors. It is so narrow that furnishings and large objects had to be hoisted up through a series of trap doors in the ceiling and floor of each room.

The inside is designed with echoes of church interiors and the richness of medieval colors. When guests enter the ground floor, there is traditional tiling to greet them, painted in an ancient process and patterned in geometric shapes that have been used by centuries of church restorers. The wallpaper here is in a Gothic pattern, and the stippled blue ceiling is reminiscent of medieval church vaults. The first floor is an office, wonderfully dramatic with its floor-to-ceiling Gothic windows. The second floor is a dining room, and the kitchen is on the third floor. There are no windows at all on this floor, so the space has been used well for storage, since cabinets would interfere with the glory of the Gothic glass found throughout the rest of the house. The bedroom on the

Tapestries appropriately adorn the stone walls of the tower, above. Here in the dining area, a sense of the medieval is brought about by an original tapestry, needlework-upholstered chairs, candles, and natural light.

fourth floor is an interesting effect in blue. It was created by applying paint in ten different glazes, then adding two layers of wax crayon, which give a hint of red and lend a three-dimensional quality to the space, making it seem bigger. In the living room on the fifth floor, light streams in through the grand yet delicate windows that frame the room. At the very top is a roof terrace that looks out on London. It is beautifully sheltered by the stone lace of the finials that form the high parapet.

The tower is not just a remarkable home, it is a reminder of an incredible history and of the brilliance of Sir Christopher Wren. To view it from the street is to understand the inscription on his tomb in St. Paul's, written by his son: "If you seek his monument, look around."

Draperies are pulled aside in the fifth-floor living room so that the windows could remain the focus of the room. The orange walls are a daring departure from the design of most living rooms, and certainly most churches.

Carriage House, *Long Island, NY*

Susanna Torre's conversion of a carriage house on the Long Island shore is a portrait in contrasts. In an eighty-year-old building that Torre describes as "at once typical and atypical," she has brought together old and new; smooth and rough textures; large, open elements and small intimate ones.

The structure was typically utilitarian—built, above all, for function—as its sensible gable roof and plain square shape testify. But it is not typical in the proportions and forms of the interior. It's obvious, Torre says, that "someone had given a great deal of thought to it." Steeply pitched roofs create wonderful slants and angles, and there are surprising corners and nooks as a result.

The carriage house was designed in 1910 by New York architect Grosvenor Atterbury; the present owners recently moved it to the seashore from an estate a quarter-mile away, where it was threatened by a planned housing development. Most of the dilapidated interior had to be gutted to convert the structure. Torre strove to

keep her additions in character with the building's Shingle Style architecture, which flourished on the Eastern seaboard when the carriage house was built, and is perfect for the building's new sandy setting. Traditional cedar was used for the shingled siding and the latticed archway at the entrance, and many of the other new elements relate to the style as well. The huge arched window at the back of the house is a contemporary interpretation of a Shingle Style form, and the new "eyebrow" balcony on the south side of the structure is also a typical motif, echoed here by a similarly shaped balcony below it. Inside, the pivotal design of the stairway—the sharp turn from one flight of stairs to another—recalls the turning interior layouts of old Shingle Style homes.

But Torre's use of Shingle Style elements is where the similarities between old and new end. Boldly contemporary elements are layered with old ones in a play of contrasts. First, there is the shift in scale between the expansive arched window at the back of the

building and the small, intimate spaces inside created by the sloping of the original walls and ceilings. This new, westward-facing "sunset window" works surprisingly well in the small building; rather than overwhelming it, the window opens it up and adds a sense of spaciousness.

Then there is the striking difference between the dramatic lines of the second story ceiling and the playful elements that Torre has added beneath it. Once the hayloft, the second floor now holds the kitchen, living and dining areas, and a few guest beds, in an "upside-down" plan that takes advantage of fine views of the ocean. The original ceiling soars and then slants in powerful angles throughout this space. But below it are new elements reminiscent of a child's tree house. The white "little house" that holds the kitchen was fit in between the angles of the ceiling, and beds were tucked into nooks on either side of it that remind one of secret hiding places.

The "little house" is a contrast in itself. With it, Torre is playing with the idea of what is interior and what is exterior, keeping the distinction between the two ambiguous by making the little structure look like an outside element—and so bringing the outside in. In fact, the entire effect of this area is of the outdoors; the grand slope of the ceiling and the exposed rafters is like the overhang of great trees, and the original brick chimney reminds Torre of a tree trunk growing out through the roof.

Another source of contrast is Torre's mix of textures. The beaded pine boards that had covered the stable ceilings now line the walls of the entry and the stair hall. These, and the areas of original exposed brick and plank floors, are intriguingly rough next to the sleek, contemporary finish of the stair rail, the smooth cedar paneling of the upstairs ceiling, and the modern white of the little house's exterior.

The theme of contrasts is distilled on the outside of the house: On one side of the building are the old stable windows and the outlines of the big doors where the carriages entered; on the others are new, undulating balconies and stretching windows that open up the building to contemporary sensibilities as well as to the outdoors. In pointing up the differences between the new and the old, Torre is inviting those who enter the building to listen to the dialogue between them—to comprehend the reality of the present while listening to the secrets of the past. They are secrets well worth being told.

The dunes and the sea are visible from the windows and upper balconies of the second floor, opposite page. The door in the large arched window serves as a separate entrance for guests staying on the upper floor. Exposed rafters, above, add to the outdoorsy feeling of this floor.

As the plan, right, shows, the bedrooms of the home are on the first floor, which allows for the more public enjoyment of the light and views of the second floor. The exterior view, below, shows the windows of the original carriage house on the first floor. These small windows accommodated the modest need for natural light in a carriage house, but were insufficient for a modern home. Architect Susana Torre modeled the new windows in the house on the originals but designed them on a larger scale.

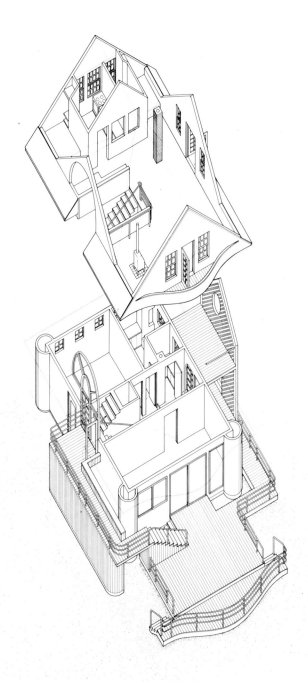

The meeting of the building's four dormers creates the distinctive angles and slants of the second-floor ceiling. This sleeping space, left, is tucked into one of the nooks created by those dramatic slants, making guests feel safe and protected.

Library, *Baltimore, MD*

There are hundred-year-old buildings to be had in Baltimore, but most of them are fourteen feet wide. In a city where row houses dominate, people brag about residences that measure sixteen feet across. Architect Peter Doo is particularly happy, in such a city, to have a home forty feet wide with twenty-five-foot ceilings. It is an old library, built in 1883 the way that city structures were built then—with lots of volume and light.

The library is one of six built at the turn of the century from the same pattern; the others still stand in the city as libraries, or have been converted to churches or community centers. But this one became a home after Doo and his wife, Barbara, noticed it

sitting vacant for months and finally convinced the city, with the community's support, to let them convert the building. It is so completely unresidential in its structure and demeanor, so municipal and public in character, that to have anyone use it as a residence at all is somewhat remarkable. As an architect friend of Doo's says, "Just the idea of putting a couch into the place is wonderful."

In effect, the couple did do little more than place a couch where the librarian's desk used to be, and moved in. Their simple approach allows the graceful spirit of the structure to show. The conservative Victorian exterior was basically left the way it was—

some paint and a few roof repairs were all that was needed structurally, and original detailing was maintained, including the stone lettering spelling out "Enoch Pratt Branch Library." (Baltimore lore has it that Mr. Pratt was responsible for giving Andrew Carnegie the idea of branch libraries, who then had them built throughout the country.) The only contemporary accent is the front door, rebuilt in the pattern of the old one that had been removed and painted bright yellow to contrast with the Victorian darkness of the rest of the exterior.

The couple found the inside of the building pretty much intact when they first entered with a flashlight. It looked dark, since the windows were boarded up, but it also looked, in Doo's words, "pretty wonderful." What attracted him was the sheer volume—2,500 square feet of it. The prospects only got better as workers uncovered the large arched windows and stripped away the plywood that protected the woodwork on the walls. (The building spent its most recent years in use as a boys' club after the library was closed, and it was boarded up to take the wear and tear.)

Underneath the boards was dirt, but also wonderful ornamental molding and detailing. The couple patched all the flat surfaces, repaired the woodworking, and painted, but they left the broken molding as it was, starting and stopping occasionally in breaks around the room. This is a charming revelation of the age of the building, and its effect is more successful than a renovation of the molding. It shows *how* the building has aged—what it has endured, what it has survived. The passage of time is made comprehensible.

A wall of windows and glass doors, opposite page, was added to separate the bedroom space from the living and dining areas. The wall provides privacy, but its transparency keeps the space connected. The building as it appeared during conversion, above: Because the windows were boarded up when architect Peter Doo first entered the building, he saw it, as he says, "in half-light." Most conversions are done with little idea of what surprise is to come next.

The one-story space was left largely open, with only two partitions added. One is the half-wall that separates the kitchen from the main living and dining areas and holds bookshelves on one side; the other is the series of glass doors and, above them, windows that close off the bedroom space. The glass partition keeps the space visually open, retaining the building's airy spirit. Through the doors is the room where the stacks once stood, and evidence of them remains—in the windows that were placed high to protect the books from the sun, in the pale marks in regular rows on the floors where the shelves shadowed over the wood and the sun couldn't darken it, as it did everywhere else. Off this space is the only separate room in the original layout—the librarian's office that now serves as the baby's room. The small room has, as Doo jokes, "only fourteen-foot ceilings" and a fireplace.

The entire building is still floored with the original "hard pine" surface. Often used in public buildings, this is wood that comes from the center of the log and is the densest, hardest, and darkest. It was left unstained to let the beauty of its years show through.

Unhampered by its residents, the natural elegance of the building shows; as Doo points out, with a good building one shouldn't have to touch much. The joy of living there comes from the structure itself more than anything that was done to it. "We can sit back and look up at the trusses," he says, "and that's really our view. It's a pleasure."

The old stone of this former Quaker meeting house is lightened up with a glass-roofed lean-to room, opposite page, placed on either side of owner Mark Wickham's artist's studio. The interior design, right, is simple to match the humble lines of the meeting house, composed of elements that were passed down or salvaged from other buildings.

Quaker Meeting House, *Devizes, England*

Mark Wickham's converted Quaker meeting house in Devizes, England, quite literally stands between the past and the present. Wickham enters the front door amid a bustle of contemporary shops, but after traveling through the house finds himself in ancient times at the back, where the door opens onto a close medieval pathway called St. John's Alley.

After years of vacancy, the building was slated to become part of a shopping mall, along with a group of surrounding buildings. In the face of this threat, some preservationist friends of Wickham's bought the buildings, then panicked when they realized they had nothing to do with them. Luckily, Wickham was looking for a place to live at the time and bought the meeting house from them, getting not only a home but a history as well.

The stalwart building was in very good condition: Having stood sturdy and sound for centuries, it was fit for more years of use and a new life. The back portion facing the alley was originally all timber before the Quakers covered it with brick, presumably to make it more structurally sound and visually impressive. The heavy stone façade that looks out on the street is a fascinating contrast to the interior, which is light, wood-lined, and comfortable.

Aside from ousting pigeons that were nesting on the stairs, all that really needed to be done on the interior was to replace a back

wall and a staircase, put in a bathroom and roof insulation, and fix up the glass "lean-to" ceilings in the kitchen and sitting room. "Someone—the Plymouth Brethren, I think—added the paneling in the Thirties," says Wickham. The Brethren knew what they were doing, because the paneling, with its humble lines, is what defines the interior. It is repeated throughout the house and serves as a vertical backdrop for the many paintings and pieces of sculpture that Wickham, an artist, has collected. His studio is in what was once the meeting hall, where the light from the original high windows, stretching almost to the ceiling, makes it seem as though the room were made to paint in.

Without exception, the furniture and fixtures within are all found. "I don't honestly think I've bought a piece of furniture since I came here. I'm lucky enough to have inherited or been given or lent exactly the right amount of oddments," says Wickham. The "oddments" sit comfortably in the building and enhance its sense of ease, among them a sash window saved from a building that was about to be demolished and an old refectory table from Marlborough College.

The little low building that stands unassumingly in Devizes High Street is the perfect haven for a working artist. "It's such a wonderfully anonymous sort of house from the outside," Wickham says. "Not many of the locals even know I'm here." Of course, in America, nothing over 200 years old is anonymous, but in England it is just another piece of history.

The low building with its curious entrance doors, opposite page, sits among busy shops of this market town. Charming touches, above, have a distinctly British flair, and are often created from pieces that have a history of their own. A sash window in the home was rescued from a building that was slated for demolition, and the dining table was taken from a college refectory.

The rooms are lit from above by windows that are positioned just below ceiling height. The studio, above, was once the main meeting hall and now is a place where oil and canvas meet. The back door, opposite page, opens onto an ancient lane. The paneling in this room is the most distinctive feature of this home, installed, it is believed, by the Plymouth brethren.

White Barn, *Chappaqua, NY*

Architect Keith Kroeger took what he calls a "discarded" barn in New York and made it into a home, thinking that after he fixed it up for fun, he would live in it for a few years and then sell it. More than a decade later, he and his wife Susan are still there after raising four children in it. Having that many children is reason enough to live in a barn, but the Kroegers had other reasons. There was the opportunity to live with the history of a building that has been around since 1837 and had been filled with hay and animals rather than a family. The barn also presented a ground for architectural experimentation, a chance for change and evolution.

Kroeger views the barn as "a great big volume with a regular structural system," a space readily adaptable to different approaches and uses. The building itself doesn't say, as Kroeger puts it, "now you are in the living room," but leaves that up to its inhabitants. The Kroegers have the house arranged so freely that they have only to move a couch or a dining room table to transport a room from one place to another. This inherent flexibility has allowed the barn to be many different things over the years: The quality of its light and its high walls rendered it the perfect setting for the art shows the Kroegers have held there; its natural acoustics and hayloft balcony have made for some great concerts; and, in its early days, when a famous actress first converted it, it served as the rehearsal hall for the local theater group.

With no balustrade, a staircase up to the hayloft master bedroom of the old barn, opposite page, continues the clean lines of the building that represent the simple life on a farm. The bed is framed by original corner beams and topped by a skylight. The "door to nowhere" to the left of the bed, fronted by Plexiglas, offers a view of the whole of the barn. Another stair without a handrail, above, connects the first and second floors.

Beams cross and join in patterns that can be seen from the bottom of the stair leading to the study, above. In a barn, though, there are really no straight edges, providing a challenge for architects. Architect Keith Kroeger delighted in the fact that "everything was crooked," and let the uneven properties of the structure show.

But even with change as a central factor in the life of the barn, its history and the spirit of its original use endures, and cannot really be escaped. This is another kind of joy for the Kroegers. They can't dig very deep in the garden without finding a horseshoe, nor renovate very far, as they did recently on the first level, without uncovering a trough strong with the wonderfully agrarian scent of manure. And there are the huge sliding barn doors on the first level where the cows came home, original wide-plank floors that are knotted and nailed and anything but refined and residential, massive rafters that emphasize the power of the structure. These elements say the building remembers its past, no matter what its present use.

Ten years ago Kroeger told real estate agents that he was looking for "a piece of junk that no one else wanted," and in this ramshackle structure, that's pretty much what he found. For him, the barn was like a big found object that he could transform into something new, while saving its essential properties. Though it had been lived in before, it had stood empty for years until a local bank took it over. While the fabric of the building was in terrible shape, the structure was sound, and the foundation was made of reinforced concrete rather than the loose stones found beneath most barns. (Horace Greeley, who lived in the area when the barn was being built, came back from Italy with news of great foundations for agrarian structures, influencing the construction of everything for miles around.) After being shown the barn, the Kroegers sat down in a restaurant and figured out on a napkin what it would

Looking out from the "door to nowhere" in the master bedroom, left, the full volume of the building becomes visible. The barn is fifty feet by thirty feet, a big rectangle divided into three floors and four bays. The study and master bedroom are on the second floor; the living room, dining room, and smaller bedrooms are on the first floor; and the lower floor, where the animals lived, is used for workspace and guest bedrooms.

cost to make the structure livable, then bought it at a bargain price from the bank, which was happy to get rid of it.

It took a lot of vision to see the beauty in a dilapidated building whose intrinsic qualities were hidden by low ceilings and a sagging—and inappropriate—front porch; they let in little light and even less of the spirit of the original structure. Kroeger stripped out the ceilings to open up the barn to its original soaring height, took off the front porch, and installed so many windows on one side of the building that it practically became a wall of glass.

Then he had the entire barn painted white—inside and out. "We really just whitewashed everything," he says. The children say it's like living in a snowstorm. Because of its simplicity and minimalism, the white lets everything in the structure show—the

beams, the rafters, the interior angles of the building are in clear view because no color or texture distracts from them.

All these changes opened up the volume of the building, and in the upper part are evocative reminders of the barn: A hay trolley that once brought hay from the loft to the floor now hangs from the ceiling; the hayloft itself, now a bedroom, still sits nearby; and light slants in through the simple barn window near the ceiling

Above all, the Kroegers appreciate the barn's lack of pretension and preciousness, its friendliness and fun. Family photographs of kids hanging off the rafters show the sheer playfulness of it. "Every time you come back to it," Kroeger says, "it somehow makes you smile." Any building that can make people smile when they walk into it was obviously well worth saving.

Another view of the staircase leading to the second floor and master bedroom, left. The polish and elegance of a piano and contemporary sculpture sit on weathered wide-plank floors. Just visible from here are the kitchen windows that Kroeger saved from buildings slated for demolition.

The barn was sited on the corner of a one-acre lot so that as much of the land as possible was available for farming. This siting is unusual; most homes are placed in the middle of lots. The barn flows down a hill in the back, opposite page, where there are original doors to another level below. A bank barn, it contained this lower floor, made possible by the landscape, for the animals to enter. The barn was red in its former life, above.

APPENDIX 1

Considerations

The Building Inspection

Before buying a building for conversion, a potential owner must first address two concerns—the structure's physical condition and its history. Full consideration of these issues will provide an overview of what to expect from an older building and can save the buyer much trouble and expense during the conversion process.

Anyone serious about purchasing an old building should hire at least one professional to help assess its condition. Architectural firms that convert structures gather a team of experts—sometimes as many as ten specialists in as many disciplines—to evaluate a project before undertaking it. For the individual buyer, an architect or a structural engineer can be invaluable (the buyer will, in all likelihood, be hiring an architect to help with the conversion, and the earlier that the architect is brought into the project the better). He or she can provide information on the soundness of the building and the extent of any structural damage, and estimate the expense of repairs (these will be in addition to the conversion costs). He or she will also be versed in local zoning restrictions and building codes, and so can advise the buyer as to the feasibility of the project.

Having hired a consultant, the potential buyer and consultant should make a thorough inspection of the building. While examining all facets of the structure, one should keep in mind that problems immediately evident often indicate more serious ones that are not apparent. No matter how thorough an inspection one undertakes, it is improbable that everything will be spotted during the initial inspection; but, with the help of the consultant, one can attempt to get a good idea of what to expect.

The following is a list of the most serious potential problems a perspective owner can expect to face from older buildings.

THE ROOF   Often the first element to show wear, the roof is generally a good indicator of the condition of a structure. A sound roof usually reflects a building in good condition. A roof that has holes in it or that is missing pieces of the roofing material, however, should be taken as a warning of other serious probable damage. A leaky roof allows water and snow to drip onto the beams, rotting them, then the floor, and so on, until it finally undermines the foundation. Is the roof complete? Is the roofing material in good shape? Are there loose, missing, or damaged shingles? Is the roof sagging? What is the condition of the drainage system?

FOUNDATION WALLS   The erosion of the foundation walls is usually indicated by the visible sagging and twisting of the building. Is this the case? Are the foundation walls cracked? Do they show other signs of erosion—particularly where the walls meet the ground?

LOCATION   The site of a building can be a cause of structural damage. In inspecting the building, the potential buyer should consider if the location of the building is apt to contribute to structural harm. For instance, a bank barn, which is set on a hill, may suffer if the hill around it is eroding. In this case, the foundation will eventually crumble with the hill. Other examples of potentially risky sites include foundations built on or near fault lines, the sea, and rivers with a history of flooding.

BEAMS, TIES, AND RAFTERS   All of these ceiling elements are vital to the structural soundness of the building. Beams, particularly those in barns, are especially important. Before the 1800s they were generally made of oak, making them stronger than the softer-wooded ones made later of fir or hemlock. However, oak beams are more susceptible to powder-post beatles that drill holes into the wood and leave evidence in the form of fine sawdust on the floor of the structure. As far as the strength of beams is concerned, if a screwdriver can be pushed into a beam, its soundness should be questioned and an expert consulted.

ABANDONED BUILDINGS   When looking into a building's background, one of the most important questions to research is the history of its occupancy. Some buildings have been abandoned for years, in which case potential owners can expect general deterioration to be as much, if not more, of a problem than structural soundness.

PLUMBING, ELECTRICITY, HEATING, AND COOLING   Repairs to these aspects of a structure may appear daunting to the potential owner, but in reality they are rarely much of a problem to install or repair these days (when done by properly skilled and accredited workmen). These kinds of repairs should not deter one from buying an otherwise sound building.

ADDITIONAL ELEMENTS   A detailed examination of the following may reveal a great deal about the condition of a building: floorboards, exposed joints, baseboards, paneling and trim, plaster work, framing members, nail holes, architectural woodwork, and wall sills.

Local Construction Laws
ZONING LAWS   In the United States, restrictions on construction are set down by local zoning boards. Local zoning laws control how many stories a building may be, how many housing units may be contructed on a given area, and so forth. A potential home-owner needs to have his or her plans approved by the regional zoning board before beginning work.

BUILDING CODES   Checking the building codes is an important preliminary step, as many are strict and very specific—and will affect how a building is transformed. Model codes serve as minimum standards for local jurisdictions that adopt them. They, like zoning laws, evolved regionally, and may be modified by and for the locality to meet its needs. There are three major codes, which, while they have many similarities, were drafted to reflect regional building differences. The model codes undergo periodic revision, and in recent years have been amended to provide greater flexibility and sensitivity for older buildings and districts. For help on understanding the codes, contact the National Conference of States on Building Codes and Standards, 481 Carlisle Drive, Herndon, VA 22101.

PRESERVATION SOCIETIES There are thousands of local preservation societies in the United States. Potential homeowners should check with the society representing the area where they hope to convert. These societies can not only be of help in researching the building and the area, but oftentimes they can suggest buildings, help converters with the Internal Revenue Service, and supply valuable information not available elsewhere.

Tax Incentives and Grants

There are no incentives from the federal government for those who convert historic structures, but there are grants and tax benefits on the state and local level. These vary widely by state and are ever-changing. Listed below are states that offered grants or incentives at the time this book went to press. More states may have enacted laws benefiting those who convert old buildings in the intervening period, and some of the laws listed may have changed. It is wise to contact the state offices for current information.

Georgia

There are some limited tax benefits for converting historic structures. For details, contact the Historic Preservation Section, 205 Butler Street, S.E., 1462 Floyd Towers East, Atlanta, GA 30334 (404) 656-2840.

Iowa

The Historical Resources Fund offers matching grants for buildings that are on the National Register and that meet the Secretary of the Interior's standards for rehabilitation. For each dollar of grant money, the owner must spend 75¢ in cash on conversion and the equivalent of 25¢ in labor or some other "soft cash" trade. Contact the Historical Resource Development Program, Bureau of Historic Preservation, Capitol Complex, Des Moines, IA 50319 (515) 281-8719.

Mississippi

It is up to the local governments in the state to determine which historic buildings should be allowed seven-year property tax increase abatements for rehabilitative work. There is also a Mississippi Landmarks program which provides other benefits. Contact the Division of Historic Preservation, P.O. Box 571, Jackson, MS 39205 (601) 359-6940.

Montana

Local programs provide a property tax abatement for the rehabilitation of buildings that are qualified for listing on the National Register. Under this program, the taxable value of the building is frozen for a five-year period at the level it was when the owners acquired it. Contact the State Historic Preservation Office, Montana Historical Society, 225 North Roberts, Helena, MT 59620 (406) 444-7715.

Nevada

Historic structures that are converted to residences are appraised as homes (for property taxes.) There is also a 38 percent property tax deferment for historic buildings. Whether or not the building qualifies is based on its age, architecture, historic features, and location. Contact the Department of Conservation and Natural Resources, Nye Building, Room 213, 201 South Fall Street, Carson City, NV 89710 (702) 885-4360.

New Mexico

For state income tax, 50 percent of eligible expenditures can be covered for the preservation and stabilization of historic buildings (this does not include new construction.) The building must be listed in the State Register of Cultural Properties; if the building is not listed, a nomination procedure can be initiated to try to get it listed. The work must be approved by the Cultural Property Review Committee, must comply with the Secretary of the Interior's standards, and must be completed within two years. This program applies to amounts up to $25,000 (at least $50,000 must be spent to qualify for $25,000). Contact the Historic Preservation Division, Office of Cultural Affairs, Villa Rivera, Room 101, 228 East Palace Avenue, Santa Fe, NM 87503 (505) 827-8320.

North Carolina

New tax laws benefiting those who convert historic buildings may be enacted. For details, contact the Division of Archives and History, Department of Cultural Resources, 109 East Jones Street, Raleigh, NC 27611 (919) 733-6547.

North Dakota

For buildings twenty-five years old or older, there is a three-year property tax exemption against the increased valuation of the building. Contact the State Historical Society of North Dakota, Heritage Center, Bismarck, ND 58505 (701) 224-2667.

Ohio

The Community Revitalization Bill provides for a break on taxes on buildings in older areas; the particular areas are declared by each community. Under this bill, property taxes are not increased as a result of work done; they remain at the same level as before rehabilitation. Contact the Ohio Historical Society, Historic Preservation Division, 1985 Velma Avenue, Columbus, OH 43211 (614) 297-2470.

Oregon

For historic buildings, there is a property tax freeze for fifteen years; for that time, the true cash value of the building remains at the pre-rehabilitation level so owners do not pay on improvements. Contact the State Parks and Recreation, 525 Trade Street, S.E., Salem, OR 97310 (503) 378-5019.

Rhode Island

There are programs being developed that benefit those who convert historic structures. For details, contact the Rhode Island Historical Preservation Commission, Old State House, 150 Benefit Street, Providence, RI 02903 (401) 277-2678.

South Dakota

For buildings on the state historic register, there is an eight-year property tax freeze, meaning that the assessment of the building cannot be increased by any approved capital investment in the structure. Contact the Office of History, South Dakota State Historical Society, 900 Governors Drive, Pierre, SD 57501 (605) 773-3458.

Virginia

There is a small grants program for the acquisition, development of plans, or rehabilitation of threatened landmarks. Buildings that qualify are judged by two criteria: the importance of the building and the seriousness of the threat to it. Contact the Department of Historic Resources, Commonwealth of Virginia, 221 Governor Street, Richmond, VA 23219 (804) 786-3143.

West Virginia

The Endangered Property Benefit allows a direct income tax checkoff. For details, contact the Department of Culture and History, Capitol Complex, Charleston, WV 25305 (304) 348-0220.

Wisconsin

For rehabilitation of historic buildings, there is a 25 percent income tax credit; the minimum expenditure must be as much as the adjusted basis of the building (purchase price minus land cost). There is a twenty-year restrictive covenant associated with this benefit, stipulating that any subsequent changes affecting the historic integrity of the building must be approved by the commission. Contact the Historic Preservation Division, State Historical Society of Wisconsin, 816 State Street, Madison, WI 53706 (608) 262-1339.

The National Trust for Historic Preservation offers a book entitled *State Tax Incentives for Historic Preservation* for $15 that covers the state laws in detail. It is available from the National Trust's Center for Preservation Policy for Studies, 1785 Massachusetts Avenue, N.W., Washington, D.C. 20036 (202) 673-4000.

Other Contacts for Tax Information

American Institute of Real Estate Appraisers
National Association of Realtors
430 North Michigan Avenue
Chicago, IL 60611
(313) 329-8559

International Association of Assessing Officers
1313 East 60th Street
Chicago, IL 60637
(312) 947-2069

American Society of Appraisers
P.O. Box 17265
Washington, D.C. 20041
(703) 478-2228

APPENDIX

2
Sources

Architects

Ann Beha Associates, Inc.
33 Kingston Street
Boston, MA 02110
(617) 338-3000

Richard Bergmann Architects
63 Park Street
New Canaan, CT 06840
(203) 966-9505

Brillembourg & Associates, Architects
30 East 67th Street
NY, NY 10021
(212) 744-9152

Centerbrook Architects and Planners
Box 409
Essex, CT 06426
(203) 767-0175

Gary M. Cunningham Architects
2700 Fairmount, Suite 200
Dallas, TX 75201
(219) 855-5272

Steven Di Meo
Old Bay Path Co. Inc.
205 Rindge Avenue
Cambridge, MA 02140
(617) 576-2685

Peter Doo
107 East Preston Street
Baltimore, MD 21202
(301) 547-8370

Frederick Fisher, Architect
2048 Broadway
Santa Monica, CA 90404
(213) 828-3663

Grattan Gill, Architect
128 Route 6A
Sandwich, MA 02563
(617) 888-4884

Bryant Glasgow, Architect
3212 West End, Suite 300
Nashville, TN 37203
(615) 386-9600

Michael Graves
341 Nassau Street
Princeton, NJ 08540
(609) 924-6409

Graham Gund Architects
47 Thorndike Street
Cambridge, MA 02141
(617) 577-9600

William Hamilton and Associates
1906 Acklen Avenue
Nashville, TN 37212
(615) 383-4974

Philetus Holt III
Holt & Morgan
350 Alexander Street
Princeton, NJ 08540
(609) 924-1358

Keith Kroeger
255 King Street
Chappaqua, NY 10514
(914) 238-5391

Louis Mackall
50 Maple Street
Branford, CT 06405
(203) 488-8364

Mark Matthews
54 Hampton Road
Southampton, NY 11968
(516) 283-5647

McInturff Architects
4220 Leeward Place
Bethesda, MD 20816
(301) 229-3705

Arthur Cotton Moore
1214 28th Street
Washington, DC 20007
(202) 337-9081

Orr & Taylor
441 Chapel Street
New Haven, CT 06511
(203) 777-3387

Redroof Design
4 East 11th Street
NY, NY 10003
(212) 598-0360

William Riesberg Architects
302 B King Street
P.O. Box 30938
Charleston, SC 29417
(803) 577-3431

Paul Rudolph
54 West 57th Street
NY, NY 10019
(212) 765-1450

William Selvage
P.O. Box 6218
Salt Lake City, UT 84106
(801) 364-0939

William Shopsin, AIA
Historical Consultant
280 West 11th Street
NY, NY 10014
(212) 989-7009

Smith-Miller & Hawkinson Architects
305 Canal Street
NY, NY 10013
(212) 966-3875

Mary Otis Stevens
Design Guild
102 South Street
Boston, MA 02111
(617) 426-0432

Susana Torre
270 Lafayette, Suite 700
NY, NY 10012
(212) 334-3625

Richard Tremaglio
5 Story Street
Cambridge, MA 02138
(617) 492-4469

Joseph Vallone Architects
155 West 19th Street, Fifth Floor
NY, NY 10011
(212) 645-1375

Peter Kurt Woerner & Associates
Architects & Builders
The Foundry
151 East Street
New Haven, CT 06511
(203) 773-1923

Designers

Leslie Claydon-White
The Millhouse
Route 6
Woodbury, CT 06798
(203) 263-3446

Nelson Ferlita
115 East 72nd Street
NY, NY 10021
(212) 288-4463

William Hodgins
232 Clarendon Street
Boston, MA 02116
(617) 262-9538

John Saladino
305 East 63rd Street
NY, NY 10021
(212) 752-2440

Builders and Carpenters

Dale Ahlum
Ahlum Construction Company
Box 446
Springtown, PA 18081
(215) 346-8550

Walter Kenul
176 Norman Avenue
Brooklyn, NY 11222
(718) 383-3667

Winans Construction
5515 Doyle Street, #9
Emeryville, CA 94608
(415) 653-7288

Peter Kurt Woerner & Associates
Architects & Builders
The Foundry
151 East Street
New Haven, CT 06511
(203) 773-1923

Architectural Salvage Yards

Architectural Antiques Exchange
709-215 N. Second Street
Philadelphia, PA 19123
(215) 922-3669

Architectural Emphasis Inc.
5701 Hollis Street
Emeryville, CA 94608
(415) 654-9520

The Architectural Salvage Co.
727 Anacapa Street
Santa Barbara, CA 93101
(805) 965-2446

Art Directions
6120 Delmar Boulevard
St. Louis, MO 63112
(314) 425-0142

Baltimore City Salvage Depot
213 W. Pratt Street
Baltimore, MD 21201
(301) 396-4599

The Bank Antiques
1824 Felicity Street
New Orleans, LA 70015
(504) 523-6055

Gargoyles Limited
512 Third Street
Philadelphia, PA 19147
(215) 629-1700

Great American Salvage Yard
3 Main Street
Montpelier, VT 05602
(802) 223-7711

Irreplaceable Artifacts
526 East 80th Street
NY, NY 10022
(212) 288-7397

Salvage One
1524 South Peoria Street
Chicago, IL 60608
(312) 733-1198

Structural Antiques
3006 N. Classen Boulevard
Oklahoma City, OK 73106
(405) 528-7734

United House Wrecking Corporation
328 Selleck Street
Stamford, CT 06920
(203) 348-5371

Urban Archaeology Ltd.
135 Spring Street
NY, NY 10012
(212) 431-6969

Webster's Landing
475-81 Oswego Boulevard
Syracuse, NY 13202
(315) 425-0142

Societies and Associations

Metropolitan Historical Commission
2nd Avenue at Broadway
Nashville, TN 37201
(615) 259-5027

The National Trust for Historic Preservation
1785 Massachusetts Avenue, N.W.
Washington, D.C. 20036
(202) 673-4000

Society for the Preservation of New
England Antiquities
141 Cambridge Street
Boston, MA 02114
(617) 227-3956

European Architects and Restorers

Gilles Bouchez and Associates
Architects
51, rue Brillat Savarin
75013 Paris France
45-81-57-41

Patrick Lorimer
Anthony Richardson and Partners
Architects and Quantity Surveyors
31 Oval Road
London NW1 7EA
England
01-485-0991

Piero Pinto
Venice Italy
41-522-2321

P.A. Terkleson Limited
Bennetts Farm
Main Street
Padbury, Bucks,
England

Miranda Tollast
The Ivy
Chippenham, Wilts,
England

Arbor, Ltd.
5 Acton Street
London WC1X 9LX
England
01-837-1192

Morgan & Oates
Church Lane
Ledbury
Herefordshire HR8 1DW
England
0531-2718

A Selection of Converted Inns

The Olde Poste Inn
43 Main Street
Cold Spring, NY 10516
(914) 265-2510

"The Barn"
1131 Grove Road
West Chester, PA 19380
(215) 436-4544

Tremont House
2300 Ship's Mechanic Row
Galveston, TX 77550
(800) 874-2300

Bibliography

Abercrombie, Stanley. *Architecture as Art*. New York: Harper & Row, 1984.

Allott, Serena. "Miracles Can Happen." *Country Homes and Interiors*, July 1986, p. 76.

Architectural Digest, all issues, 1981–1988.

Barna, Joel Warren. "Power House." *Progressive Architecture*, December 1988, p. 88.

Bethany, Marilyn. "Move-In Condition." *New York*, June 11, 1984, p. 61.

Diamonstein, Barbaralee. *Remaking America*. New York: Crown Publishers, Inc., 1986.

Gallivan, Joan Fisch. "Belle Meade Metamorphosis." *Southern Accents*, March/April 1989, p. 120.

Giovanni, Joseph. "Living in a Former Church: Space, Drama, and Tranquility." *The New York Times*, March 7, 1985.

Gray, Marlene, "An Empty Barn and a Fantasy." *The Boston Globe*, July 5, 1985.

Home, all issues, 1982–1988.

House and Garden, all issues, 1982–1988.

Howe, Rob. "The Rescue of a Roomy 1840s Barn." *Washington Home*, November 14, 1985.

Lasdun, Denys, editor. *Architecture in an Age of Scepticism*. New York: Oxford University Press, 1984.

Leonard, Brian. "The Round House." *Country Living*, April 1989, p. 104.

MacDonald, Sandy. "A Room of One's Own: Robert Indiana's Odd Fellows Lodge." *New England Monthly*, March 1987, p. 56.

Margolies, Jane. "Rustic Moves Upscale." *House Beautiful*, November 1988, p. 88.

Metropolitan Home, all issues, 1985–1986.

Miller, Donald L., editor. *The Lewis Mumford Reader*. New York: Pantheon Books, 1986.

National Trust for Historic Preservation. *All About Old Buildings*. Washington, D.C.: The Preservation Press, 1985.

National Trust for Historic Preservation. *Respectful Rehabilitation*. Washington, D.C.: The Preservation Press, 1982.

The New York Times Magazine, all issues, 1984–1987.

Oberwager, Laurence E. "Back to School." *Decorating and Remodeling*, March 1989, p. 82.

Ryder, Sharon Lee. "Off the Beaten Path: Homes Thrive in Quirky Spaces." *The New York Times*, October 13, 1988.

Shopsin, William C. *Restoring Old Buildings for Contemporary Uses*. New York: Whitney Library of Design, 1986.

Smolen, M. "Carriage House Conversion." *New Shelter*, February 1986, p. 79.

Snyder, Tim. "Dutch Reformed." *Harrowsmith*, October 1988, p. 62.

Wolfe, Tom. *From Bauhaus to Our House*. New York: Farrar, Straus & Giroux, 1981.

Zander, Peter. "Church Revival." *Fine Homebuilding*. February/March 1983, p. 67.

Photo Credits

Barbara Anello, *42*

Tim Beddow/Syndication International Ltd., *47, 48*

Richard Bergmann FAIA, *7 (above right)*, *8, 24, 114, 118, 120 (2), 121*

Gilles Bouchez, *16*

Robert Emmett Bright, *3, 12, 13, 15*

Peter Doo, *143*

Christopher Drake/Syndication International Ltd., *80–83*

Michael Dunne/Elizabeth Whiting Associates, *5, 6, 128–131, 132 (2), 133*

Tony Giammarino, *135, 136, 138 (left)*

Grattan Gill, *26*

Bryant Glasgow, *99*

Rob Gray, *62–65, 67, 115, 117, 152–158*

Brent Herridge, *37, 54*

Jonathan Hillyer. Copyright by *Southern Accents*, Inc. March/April 1989. Reprinted with permission. *31, 46, 96–98, 100 (2), 101*

Warren Jagger, *84 (left)*, *85–88*

Walter Kenul, *66*

Susan Kroeger, *159*

The Landmark Trust, *25, 27, 39*

© 1988 Andrew D. Lautman, *123*

Norman McGrath, *52*

Mark McInturff, *125, 126 (below right)*

© Jeff McNamara 1989, *7 (below right)*, *50, 74–78, 79 (2)*

Jeff McNamara. Reprinted from *Metropolitan Home* magazine, © Copyright, Meredith Corporation, 1985. All rights reserved. *122, 124*

James Merrell/Syndication International Ltd., *146–151*

Michael Nicholson/Elizabeth Whiting Associates, *43*

Robert Perron, *10, 11, 14, 18, 19, 23, 32, 38, 45, 53*

Spike Powell/Elizabeth Whiting Associates, *22, 68–72, 73 (2)*

Retep Renreow, *7 (left)*, *57*

© J. Brough Schamp 1989, *140–142, 144, 145*

Roberto Schezen, *34, 41*

William Seitz, *20, 56, 58–60*

D. Mark Simmons, *33, 160*

Jessica Strang, *90–93, 94 (2), 95*

Tim Street-Porter, *36, 49*

Sam Sweezy, *28, 30*

Karen Tanaka, *127*

Jim Tingstrum, *102–105*

Stefan Tur, *21*

Deidi von Schaewen, *17, 40, 44*

James F. Wilson, *29, 51, 55, 106–112, 113 (2)*

Tom Yee. Courtesy *House & Garden*. Copyright © 1982 by The Condé Nast Publications Inc., *35, 134, 137, 139*

Architectural Drawing Credits

Peter Anders, *138 (right)*

Richard Bergmann Architects, *116, 119*

Cunningham Architects, *113*

Graham Gund Architects, *84 (right)*, *89*

Mark McInturff, *126 (above left)*

Peter Kurt Woerner & Associates AIA, *61*

Index